EILERT SUNDT

On Marriage in Norway

TRANSLATED AND INTRODUCED BY

MICHAEL DRAKE
The Open University

CAMBRIDGE UNIVERSITY PRESS

CAMBRIDGE

LONDON   NEW YORK   NEW ROCHELLE

MELBOURNE   SYDNEY

Published by the Press Syndicate of the University of Cambridge
The Pitt Building, Trumpington Street, Cambridge CB2 1RP
32 East 57th Street, New York, NY 10022, USA
296 Beaconsfield Parade, Middle Park, Melbourne 3206, Australia

First published in Norwegian as *Om Giftermaal i Norge* 1855

First published in English, with a new introduction, by
the Cambridge University Press 1980
English edition © Cambridge University Press 1980

Printed in Great Britain by
Western Printing Services Ltd, Bristol

British Library Cataloguing in Publication Data
Sundt, Eilert
On marriage in Norway.
1. Marriage – Norway – History – 19th century
I. Title II. On marriage in Norway
301.42′09481   HQ645   79–42648

ISBN 0 521 23199 X

Contents

of people in the aforementioned age group has, as was to be
expected, slowly eased: witness the favourable conditions in
the country in the years 1851–55 (para. 101). But it can be
foreseen that in the not too distant future, in the years around
1870, a situation similar to that of 1841–50 will, in all probability occur once again (para. 102). Besides the difficulty of
obtaining a living, rising expectations also contributed to de-
laying entry into marriage, and that too within the working
class (para. 103–4).

In retrospect: the chief reason for the changes in marital
conditions, and the subordinate reasons (para. 105–7).

The importance of learning about the great many differences
in the lives of the people (para. 108–11). The explanation given
for the marked increase in the number of marriages in the
period 1841–50 applies also to the individual deanery districts
(para. 112–15). The frequency of marriage least in the districts
from which out-migration takes place, greatest on the other
hand where in-migration occurs. This lends support to the
view of decreasing recklessness in the establishment of marriages (para. 116–18). Further examination of marriage frequency in the individual deanery districts (para. 119–20).
Marriage frequency in the five dioceses and in Gudbrandsdalen (para. 121–2).

Private communication from the parish priests of the Christiania and Christiansand dioceses concerning marriage in the
propertied and working classes (para. 123–7). The number of
marriages in each of the two classes (para. 128). Intermarriage
between the upper and lower classes (para. 129–30). Bachelors
and widowers, spinsters and widows (para. 131). The age at
marriage of bachelors and spinsters in each class (para. 132–3).
The bridegrooms of the propertied class older than those of the
working class; but the brides of the former, younger than those
of the latter (para. 134–6). Why it is that young men in the
two classes marry at different ages. Why the men of the propertied class take so much younger wives (para. 141–4), whilst
the men of the working class choose wives from amongst the
somewhat older girls (para. 145–9). Observations about night
courtship (para. 150). An example of a very circumspect marriage within the working class (para. 151).

Figures and Tables

FIGURES

TABLES

The dioceses and deaneries of Norway *c.* 1850.

Acknowledgements

Of those who helped me produce this translation I would like to give an especial thanks to Dr Sølvi Sogner, the Historical Institute, University of Oslo for her continuous encouragement; the Norwegian Research Council for Science and the Humanities for financial assistance; Geraldine Stoneham for improving the quality of the text and to the staff of Cambridge University Press; Nicky Salter for typing the first draft and Sandy Jennings for typing the second. The shortcomings that remain are mine alone.

Introduction

Eilert Sundt's work is as remarkable today as it was in his own lifetime. He tackled problems of great moment: poverty, delinquency, demographic change, minority groups, the role of women, working class education. He is recognized within Norway as a pioneer of sociology and social anthropology. For economic, demographic and social historians he produced a mass of data, both quantitative and qualitative, covering all aspects of life in what was still an essentially peasant society, overwhelmingly rural and just on the threshold of industrialization. His empirical studies can be likened to those of Henry Mayhew, Le Play or Charles Booth. More recently it has been argued that 'the time is now ripe to launch Sundt as a theoretician, as a contemporary of Marx and a forerunner of Durkheim'.[1] (His work on suicide, for instance, with its insistence on the primary importance of social control, is a theme later taken up by the latter.)[2] He is said to have been one of the first in any country to apply Darwin's theory of natural selection to social phenomena, though he was no crude Social Darwinist.[3] Above all, for an age that is filled with doubt about the limitations of discipline-based research Sundt's 'enormous and infectious intellectual curiosity',[4] which knew no such blinkers, is a source of tremendous inspiration. He ranged far and wide from 1850, when his first book (*An Account of the Gypsy People in Norway*) appeared, to the publication of his last work (*On Domestic Life in Norway*) in 1873.

Enthusiasm for Sundt even within his native Norway, is of comparatively recent origin. Outside he remains virtually unknown. One wonders what his reputation would have been had the French translation of that first book (made shortly after its appearance in Norway) been

---

[1] Jon Elster, *Dagbladet*, 30 October 1978.
[2] Nils Christie, *Eilert Sundt som fanteforsker og sosialstatistiker*, University of Oslo, Institutt for Sosiologi, Oslo, 1958, p. 15.
[3] Elster, *Dagbladet*.
[4] *ibid.*

printed.[5] As it happened, from 1869, when the State stopped his funds, thus effectively bringing his research to an end, to the 1950s, there was only sporadic interest shown in his work. Somewhat ironically, as Nils Christie observed, there was much in the way of theory and technique that could have been taken direct from Sundt, but in fact came to Norway via American social science textbooks after the Second World War.[6] Recently, however, there have been reprints in paperback of a number of his works[7] and in 1978, in a major publishing venture, the last of 11 volumes covering most of his major output appeared.[8]

Eilert Sundt was born on 8 August 1817 in Farsund, a small town on the south-west coast of Norway which, at that time, had a population of about 600. His father, a one-time ship's captain, but by then a small shopkeeper, had difficulty in rearing his large family; Eilert was the last of 13. Fortunately his mother belonged to the ranks of the indomitable, turning her hand to a wide range of activities, each bringing in a little money.[9] It was not enough, however, to keep Eilert at school and from the age of 12–14 years he was self-taught.[10] Neverthe-

[5] Helge Refsum, 'Sundt', *Norsk Biografisk Leksikon*, p. 279.
[6] Christie, *Eilert Sundt*, p. 13.
[7] *Om giftermål i Norge*, Universitetsforlaget, Oslo, 1967; *Harham. Et eksempel fra fiskeridistrikterne*, Universitetsforlaget, Oslo, 1971; *Om Piperviken og Ruseløkbakken*, Tiden, Oslo, 1968; *Om saedelighedstilstanden i Norge*, 2 vols., Pax, Oslo, 1968; *Beretning om fante-eller landstrygerfolket i Norge*, Universitetsforlaget, Oslo, 1974.
[8] The books, all published by Gyldendal Norsk Forlag, Oslo, are:
    vol. 1 *Fante-eller landstrygerfolket i Norge (The gypsies of Norway)*.
    vol. 2 *Om dødeligheden i Norge (On mortality in Norway)* and *Om giftermål i Norge (On marriage in Norway)*.
    vol. 3 *Om Røros og omegn (On Røros and district)*; *Om Piperviken og Ruseløkbakken (On Piperviken and Ruseløkbakken)* and *Harham. Et eksempel fra fiskeridistrikterne (Harham: a case study from the fisheries)*.
    vol. 4 *Om saedeligheds-tilstanden i Norge (On morality in Norway)*.
    vol. 5 *Om aedruelighed-tilstanden i Norge (On temperance conditions in Norway)*.
    vol. 6 *Om bygnings-skikken på landet i Norge (On building practices in the rural areas of Norway)*.
    vol. 7 *På havet (On the sea)*.
    vol. 8 *Om husfliden i Norge (On cottage industry in Norway)*.
    vol. 9 *Om renligheds-stellet i Norge (On cleanliness in Norway)*.
    vol. 10 *Om huslivet i Norge (On domestic life in Norway)*.
    vol. 11 *Om fattigforholdene i Christiania (On poverty in Christiania)*.
[9] These and other biographical details are taken from H. O. Christophersen, *Eilert Sundt; en dikter i kjensgjerninger*, Gyldendal Norsk Forlag, Oslo, 1962, *passim*; also Michael Drake, *Population and Society in Norway 1735–1865*, Cambridge University Press, Cambridge, 1969, pp. 19–29. It is not altogether unlikely that Sundt's oft-repeated claim that women frequently played a dominant role in the running of many Norwegian households, especially those of the crofters, owes something to his own childhood experience. See below, pp. 160–1.
[10] Refsum, 'Sundt', p. 277.

less, backed by his doughty mother who was determined to see one of her sons join the Norwegian Lutheran clergy, Sundt entered the university in Christiania (now Oslo), having come top of the 132 candidates who sat the university entrance examination in 1835. Thus he entered a milieu swept by waves of national feeling, the first generation to reach university after independence from 400 years of Danish rule in 1814. He calls it the 'radical generation' (see below, pp. 98, 108) committed to freedom, romantically attached to all things Norwegian.

Partly because of illness, partly through an unwillingness to face the choice of a career (not unknown amongst students today), Sundt did not graduate until 1846. He might have chosen a straightforward career in the Church (he had pursued a theological line of study) or the university. In fact he did become, briefly, a fellow in ecclesiastical history. He was, however, 'thinking of something else than following the beaten road of routine living'.[11] Taking a Sunday school class in Christiania prison, he noticed an inmate 'with hair, beard and burly eyebrows as black as a raven's and a skin...of a darker hue than one finds on a normal sunburned Norwegian face'.[12] The man turned out to be a gypsy, confined to prison for not having voluntarily presented himself for instruction leading to confirmation in the State Church. From this chance meeting Sundt began his studies of the gypsies for which he later received financial assistance from the government. The authorities were so impressed by his work that not only did they publish it at public expense, but also, in the autumn of 1850, gave him a grant so that he might pursue his studies into the condition of the Norwegian lower classes. It was to last for one year and was the first of a series of annual grants which continued until 1869. Few governments have reaped such a rich return on their investment in social scientific research; none have got so much from the work of one man.

Sundt began what turned out to be his life's work at a time of considerable social unrest. Norway had escaped serious disturbances in the revolutionary year 1848, but the authorities had been shaken by the growth of a radical socialist movement led by Marcus Thrane, a newspaper editor. Much of the inspiration for this came from the English Chartists. At its height it was to be the biggest socialist movement in the world, reckoned in relation to the country's population. Sundt was appalled by its revolutionary tenor and because it set Norwegians

11 Cited in Martin S. Allwood, *Eilert Sundt. A Pioneer in Sociology and Social Anthropology*, Oslo, Olaf Norlis Forlag, 1957, p. 22.
12 Cited in Christophersen, *Eilert Sundt*, p. 68.

against one another. He joined the movement, however, with the intention of depoliticizing it.[13] In this he failed. The government then used
force, arresting Thrane in 1851 (he was to remain in prison until 1858)
and other leaders. The movement's collapse was aided by improving
economic conditions. *On Marriage in Norway* contains several references
to what Sundt calls the Workers' Agitation (see below, pp. 94, 102).
He undoubtedly sympathized with the plight of the lower classes (p. 99)
but as a believer in the ability of a free society (p. 107) and of economic
growth[14] to solve their problems (p. 105 and n. 3, p. 102) he could not
support their methods. For him revolution was not the answer, but
progress was both possible and likely. Sundt was no Malthusian
(p. 99). There is little in the Sundt of 1850 to distinguish him from
most other members of his class. Like them he subscribed to a set of
moral values which led him to condemn many of the actions of the
working class. Some of these he discusses in *On Marriage in Norway*,
including early marriage, illegitimate births and 'night courtship'
(bundling). But even as early as 1855, when that book appeared, Sundt
is seen to have changed his views markedly. He says that much in our
actions is socially determined: 'what is permissible and right, what is
decent and becoming. These ideas and opinions embrace us tightly on
all sides, like the water in which the fish swim, like the air in which the
birds fly' (p. 53). What appears right and proper to one group in
society appears scandalous to another. He notes, for instance, that the
urban middle class regarded night courtship as highly offensive (so
much so that Sundt comments on his daring in having written about it
more openly than anyone had ever done). And yet the offence this
causes the urban population is no greater than that felt by country folk
at the sight of a kiss between engaged or married couples (p. 162).
He discusses the impact of work on the determination of ideas and
values (p. 115) and sees much of the differences in the latter, between
one part of the country and another, as a product of different work
situations. He warns against 'judging a single feature of lower-class life
when one does not know the whole' (p. 158). Thus, for example, to
condemn, as morally reprehensible, the crofter's son for marrying at
a comparatively early age (the outcry against the supposed 'reckless
marriages' was the starting point of Sundt's study) was to ignore the
economic and social context which, when understood, revealed the

[13] Anne-Lise Seip, 'Forholdet mellom "Capitalen og Arbeidet" i gruvesamfunnet
Røros 1851', *Historisk Tidsskrift*, 53:4, 1975, pp. 392–3.
[14] Anne-Lise Seip 'Eilert Sundt og vekstideologiens dillemma', *Historisk Tidsskrift*,
54:4, 1975, pp. 316–46.

action as being the most rational (and morally justifiable) in the circumstances. The more Sundt studied, the more he understood and the more
he came to justify the actions of working-class Norwegians. By putting
oneself into the circumstances of the poor one is less inclined to condemn their actions, he writes at the close of *On Marriage in Norway*
(p. 162). Between 1850 and 1869 Sundt moved from trying to get the
working class to accept the values of the middle class to seeking to
justify the former to the latter. At times he appeared to be defending
the indefensible. To the liberal progressives whose platform he had
once shared he appeared hopelessly reactionary. This in part explains
the abrupt and ignominious end to his life's work when in 1869 the
Norwegian parliament passed a motion to end his grant (by 51 votes
to 47). In part too it explains why he had no immediate followers.

   On Marriage in Norway produced Sundt's widely known theoretical
insight – 'Sundt's Law' as the Swedish statistician Axel Gustav
Sundbärg dubbed it.[15] How he came to discover this is described by
Sundt in almost lyrical terms (p. 21). In essence he argued that the
sharp increase in marriages in the 1840s (24 per cent up on the 1830s)
was, to a great extent, independent of the economic circumstances of
the time or of any change in moral conditions (an increased recklessness and improvidence on the part of the poor was often alleged);
rather it was a product of a baby boom in the decade after 1815 which
led to a massive increase of almost 40 per cent in the 20–30-year-old
age group between 1835 and 1845. This baby boom of the post-
Napoleonic period was, in its turn, not a product of the circumstances
of that time, but of an earlier surge in the birth rate in the 1790s. Sundt
traced this wave-like movement back as far as records permitted – to
the 1740s. The discovery was both novel and important. Novel because
however much Sundt combed the Norwegian and the foreign literature
(pp. 24–9 and 66, 91–2 n. 7) he could find no support for it, important
because it exposed the crassness of much of the conventional wisdom
on the subject as articulated by the middle class. Relative to the size of
the marriageable age groups, the numbers of marriages actually declined
in the 1840s, whilst the age at marriage rose. All talk of recklessness on
the part of the working class with regard to establishing a marriage
should now be done away with, argued Sundt. 'It has nothing to do
with reality: it is an unjustifiable exaggeration' (p. 141). Sundt also
showed that although the average age at first marriage of working-class
Norwegian men (mostly crofters and day-labourers) was lower than

[15] Refsum, 'Sundt', p. 281.

that of the propertied class (i.e. the farmers) there was little in it (28.2 years as against 29.7) and, in any case, neither could be regarded as early.[16] More importantly Sundt discovered that the brides of the working class were, on average, older than those of the propertied class, namely 26.8 years as against 25.9 years (p. 143). Sundt's discovery and explanation of these differences represent a signal contribution to our understanding of this important element of socio-demographic behaviour. Methodologically the demonstration of his law caused Sundt to break new ground in developing cohort analysis, despite having only crude data at his disposal (pp. 59–74).

The importance of Sundt's Law was not confined to his own day nor to his own country – though he admitted it did more to explain Norwegian conditions (and to a lesser degree those of Denmark and Sweden) than it did those of the major European countries such as England, France and Prussia (p. 9). The western world today is very conscious of the impact of past changes in fertility – of baby booms and slumps – on social and economic developments. The following extract from a recent article is very reminiscent of *what* Sundt wrote 125 years earlier, though hardly of *how* he wrote.

Note how the low growth of labour force in the 1950s and high growth in the 1960s and 1970s echo the birth rate 20 years earlier. . . . Whereas before World War II, swings in labour supply were largely influenced by aggregate demand conditions, swings in the labour supply now occur largely independently of aggregate demand conditions. . . . Thus a swing in the birth rate generates a shock wave that shows up through time in the changing age structure of the population. . . . When young adults are in increasingly short supply, their labour market situation improves, and their relative well-being increases: when they are in growing surfeit, their labour market situation deteriorates, and their relative well-being diminishes. A growth in relative well-being encourages earlier marriages and child bearing; conversely, when relative well-being deteriorates, marriage and child-bearing are postponed.[17]

[16] Sundt's social classification system, on his own admission, is rudimentary (p. 135) and has attracted criticism, e.g. Ståle Dyrvik, 'Om giftarmål og sosiale normer: ein studie av Etne 1715–1801', *Tidsskrift for samfunnsforskning*, vol. 11, 1970, p. 294. Nevertheless, crude though it may be, it does produce results – especially on the crucial question of differences in age at marriage – that have been, broadly speaking, borne out by other studies. Dyrvik, *op. cit.* p. 296, for instance, found that in the period 1755–94 the mean age at first marriage of bridegrooms in the farming class was 28.8 years as against 28.7 for those in the crofter class. The respective ages of their brides were 25.2 years and 29.9. See also Drake, *Population and Society*, pp. 124–32.

[17] Richard M. Easterlin, Michael L. Wachter, and Susan M. Wachter, 'Demographic influences on economic stability: the United States experience', *Population and Development Review*, IV:1, 1978, pp. 7, 9, 16.

If Eilert Sundt's interests were wide-ranging, so too were the methods he used to explore them. *On Marriage in Norway* exemplifies this. So much so that it can be studied as a manual of research methods in the social sciences, with the added virtue of readability thrown in! Sundt set up hypotheses and tested them. For this he drew on the writings of other scholars, both native and foreign (pp. 24, 66). He used historical data derived from parish registers of births, marriages and deaths as well as earlier censuses. He even tried his hand at what today would be called oral history, though somewhat ruefully he writes that 'although the Norwegian farmer is remarkably conversant with present conditions in his parish, indeed almost within each and every house, his knowledge is very imperfect and confused about the conditions and events of earlier times' (p. 21). He had a strong commitment to quantitative analysis, arguing, in the particular context of this book, that the 'purpose of giving statistical information about the condition of the people is so that this will guide our investigations into the life of the people'. To answer a question not with guesses and impressions based on chance examples, but with figures was always at the forefront of Sundt's methodology. That is not to say he did not believe in the value of qualitative evidence derived from first-hand contact, conversations and interviews. During the six and a half years from December 1850 to the summer of 1857, Sundt reckoned that his research caused him to be travelling for 754 days.[18] He talked to farmers, crofters, labourers, teachers, civil servants, clergy, factory owners, indeed anyone who would help throw light on what interested him. In *On Marriage in Norway*, Sundt makes especial mention of one of his informants, a farmer, with whom he had a conversation that 'lasted from morning till night for an entire eight days!' Sundt was also a great exponent of the use of the questionnaire. Several of his books depend very heavily on material acquired in this way; for example his three-volume *Om saedeligheds-tilstanden i Norge* (*On morality in Norway*) as well as his *Om aedruelígheds-tilstanden i Norge* (*On temperance conditions in Norway*). For the latter exercise Sundt sent out 2,431 questionnaires (one for each school district) requesting information on the level of sobriety in the area. He had 2,008 returned.[19] His subsequent analysis of these for possible shortcomings has been described as still today 'a joy to read'.[20] His questionnaire for *On Marriage in Norway* was a more modest affair, being sent only to the

[18] Christophersen, *Eilert Sundt*, p. 97.
[19] *ibid.* p. 174.
[20] Christie, *Eilert Sundt*, p. 12.

197 parish priests of the Christiania and Christiansand dioceses. The questionnaire itself, however, was far from modest, containing as it did 109 items. It was completed by 158 priests (p. 134).

Sundt was both an academic and a politician.[21] In some ways he can be likened to the members of the British statistical movement of the 1830s and 1840s.[22] Sound reform could and must be based on sound 'facts'. Only then could the proper policies be pursued. Though the aspiration may have been naive, the research it led to was far from being so. Sundt also wanted to share his knowledge, to take his people with him, not to use it to legislate from on high. To this end he tried to present his findings in as readable a form as possible. The task was a daunting one as he and many who have tried since have discovered. 'I have written in a style that is not the kind usually used in these so-called statistical essays. I aim to write so that the ordinary man, whom I know is not accustomed to reading this kind of work, will be able to read it without too great difficulty or boredom' (p. 7). He takes great pains to talk his readers through his figures and tables. Indeed so successful is he in this that the beginning social scientist with a fear of numbers might well overcome it should he choose to follow Sundt through this book. His use of extended metaphors is another key element of his writing style, as is his use of anecdotes. The stories of Per and Anne, Ole and Karen, of Jacob Shoemaker and Marit Hansdatter are in some cases true stories, in others anecdotes devised by Sundt from a series of experiences. But he is scrupulous in stating which is which. As befits a mid-nineteenth-century clergyman *On Marriage in Norway* contains a number of religious passages. They are conventional in character and on occasion rather stilted, as if presented in the line of duty rather than with any depth of feeling or commitment.[23]

How successful was Sundt in reaching the public he sought? Most of his work came out either within the pages of *Folkevennen* (The People's Friend) or as supplements to it. This journal was founded in 1852 as the organ of Selskabet for Folkeoplysningens Fremme (The Society for the Promotion of Popular Enlightenment) which began its work in the same year. Sundt was a member of the Society's committee in 1852 and became its chairman and editor of its journal in 1858. By 1862, the circulation of *The People's Friend* had risen to 4,277 (of which 11 copies went overseas); a remarkable total given that the

[21] Seip, 'Forholdet mellom "Capitalen og Arbeidet" i gruvesamfunnet', p. 389.
[22] See M. J. Cullen, *The Statistical Movement in Early Victorian Britain: The Foundations of Empirical Social Research*, Hassocks, Harvester Press, 1975.
[23] Seip, 'Sundt og vekstideologiens dillemma', p. 320 also makes this point though she lays greater emphasis on Sundt's religious values.

population of the country was then only 1.6 millions. In that year Sundt carried out an analysis of the circulation list.[24] Of the 4,266 Norwegian subscribers the largest single group was made up of farmers (634), the smallest of crofters or cottars (*husmenn*) who numbered 6. There were 425 senior civil servants and professional people, 310 priests, 156 officers, 396 school teachers, training college students and parish clerks. In addition to these individual members, 495 libraries also took the journal. Regionally *The People's Friend* was fairly evenly distributed with the exception of the Christiansand Diocese in the south-west of the country and the Tromsø Diocese in the far north which had approximately 60 per cent and 70 per cent of the national average respectively, calculated on a per head of the population basis. Despite the fact that Norway was overwhelmingly rural at this time (only 16 per cent lived in urban areas in 1865) half the subscribers lived in the towns. Neither the society, nor its journal, quite lived up to its name, as Sundt admitted.[25] Those cottars and poor farmers who appear in the pages of *On Marriage in Norway* would rarely appear to have read about themselves in the pages of *The People's Friend*. Workers' education movements still, of course, share this same fate.

Eilert Sundt became parish priest of Eidsvoll in 1870. Thus at the age of 53 he began the career for which he had been trained a quarter of a century earlier. Economically he was better off than he had ever been. Eidsvoll was a good living. But the ending of his research grant in 1869 deeply disappointed him. When he died in 1875 he left behind an enormous corpus of works ranging from major studies in demography, sociology, social anthropology and ethnography to masterly vignettes covering only a few pages, for example, his analysis of the position of some handsawyers facing the competition of the steam-driven saw[26] or his examination of politeness amongst the farming population of Guldalen, a parish in the Throndhjem Diocese.[27] These, and the non-political Worker's Association of Christiania were his legacy. Not until the 1960s did he get a physical monument commensurate with his stature, when the spanking new social science faculty building at the University of Oslo was named – Eilert Sundt's House.

---

[24] Eilert Sundt, 'Om vort selskab', *Folkevennen*, 11, 1862, pp. 568–80.
[25] Eilert Sundt, 'Folkevennens første ti Aar', *Folkevennen*, 10, 1861, p. 646.
[26] Eilert Sundt, 'Arbeidsvesen.i.Haandsagen', *Folkevennen*, 13, 1864, pp. 329–40.
[27] Eilert Sundt, 'Bygde-skikke Første stykke', *Folkevennen*, 7, 1857, pp. 17–56.

I

Different points of view

1 It was a fine day in the autumn of 1853. I was walking in a wooded district, some forty kilometres from Christiania, amongst a group of crofters' cottages and small-holdings that belonged to some large farms. On one of these small-holdings the middle-aged wife of the crofter was engaged in carrying potatoes into the living-room and there tumbling them through the trap-door into the cellar. A couple of adolescent girls were helping her, but her husband was away working on his master's farm. I was tired and sat down until the woman finished her work and gave herself up to talk with me. We had not set eyes upon each other before, but were soon, so to speak, acquainted. She regaled me with some apples from a fine tree, between the leaves of which the sun shone through the living-room window. This tree had not been planted by the crofter but by his predecessor, a queer old bachelor. However it was quite apparent that the present family were happy to have beautiful and pleasant things around them. I took a real delight in looking around me. For the first time in a crofter's living-room I noticed a four-poster bed with russet curtains. The Swedish clock hung in the corner, and, against the one long wall, there was a large chest of drawers, which I could not help thinking was well filled with all kinds of good things, witness to the wise housewife's industry and prudence. It was evidently a fairly prosperous household, although they had had four or five children to rear, and everything that I learned about their domestic life taught me to respect them as worthy folk.

I asked the woman how long they had been married, and she told me. At another point in our conversation I discovered how old the couple now were. A small calculation then gave me their age at marriage. They were very young, 21 or 22 years old. I mentioned this to the woman, and she shook her head over the folly of youth.

'Both of you, perhaps, were crofters' children?'

Yes, they were.

'And I suppose you were in service before you came together?'

Yes, at that time it was the usual thing for the children of poor people.

'Perhaps you were also in service together on the same farm?'

No, not quite, but they weren't far apart.

'Now I think I see how it all came about. But tell me, my dear woman, since you certainly hadn't great wealth from home, and you couldn't have collected much during the short time you were in service, had you anything to begin with when you were married? I know that people intending to keep house should have this and that, but what could you have?'

Oh, it was little indeed that they had.

'Yes, but you still must have had something?'

No, it was right enough. They had absolutely nothing.

'But my dear, wasn't that really very strange?'

'Yes, but I did have a wooden spoon,' the woman replied.

'A wooden spoon?' I repeated.

'Yes, and I got it from Anne Rogneby, the last woman I worked for. It happened that just when I was about to leave her service, it was when the banns were being read from the pulpit, she said: "I think you had better take this wooden spoon with you, Karen, for then at least you will have something to eat with when you and Ole marry." I didn't pay much attention to the wooden spoon then, for I was crying so much. But I said thank you, and it came in very handy. For when we were married, Ole and me, I had a wooden spoon, but he hadn't!'

'Hadn't he even a wooden spoon?' I exclaimed. 'Had he then a place to live in, or cups, kitchen utensils, a cooking-pot? And had he anything to give you to cook in the pot?'

'Him?'

No, was the reply to all these questions. However, for the first six months they had permission to live in a cottage belonging to some of the woman's relations. There she got the loan of a cooking pot. For the first meal she should cook, she had no flour. But Ole had his grandmother living on a pension in a cottage in the neighbourhood. He went to her, got some fistfuls of flour, 'and carried them right home in his hat'.

I was forced to smile at the woman's simple-hearted tale. But even more was I forced to wonder and delight at the great munificence of the Heavenly Father, who provides for his many, many children, both for the care-free and the troubled. And I know for sure that my readers cannot be anything but pleased that all still went well with Ole and

Karen, though their happy-go-lucky beginning had hardly augured well.

2 That beginning was not auspicious. For indeed here was one of those marriages which we must say are contracted without thought, 'a folly of youth', as Karen herself said. And amongst people who, tempting God, begin their domestic life in such a way, there are to be found many examples that show how unhappily it can work out, both for the parents and for the children 'unto the third generation'. These young, thoughtless, inexperienced people marry in poverty, and soon, perhaps, have about them a numerous brood of children, whom they can neither feed nor clothe properly, nor, since they are even less possessed of wisdom and understanding, bring up in the love and fear of the Lord. In the next generation, one can see that the one house of the poor and brutalized has begot and filled many houses, from which, perhaps, despair surveys the country round and vice goes out to plunder.

3 The fact that so many of the country's sons and daughters marry in wretchedness, and by their thoughtlessness increase the community's burden of trouble, has been, and still is, a subject of great concern for many serious and well-disposed citizens. And many intelligent men, who have lived right in the midst of the people and so have had a good opportunity to observe their habits and customs, have even come to the opinion that this is something which in the last generation has become worse rather than better.

In the countryside in particular, where, for various reasons, this matter is a subject of much attention and debate, I have often heard worthy and knowledgeable men express themselves thus: 'It was bad before but it's become even worse since the new poor law of 1845. For that gives the poor the right to claim help whenever anything goes wrong. And now it's come to the point when the poorest boy who, perhaps, only a few years ago was entirely dependent upon the charity of his neighbours and who even now has not been long enough in service to get full wages, thinks there is no problem about getting married. So he goes to the priest and requests that the banns be published and the wedding solemnized, for he can always find a girl who thinks the same way as he does.' Other people go further back in time and look at the matter more profoundly. One of the poor's best friends, a worthy man who, despite his grey hairs, occupies an official position of great trust and honour, told me that in his opinion: 'It is the spirit of the age. It is the ideas of the French Revolution – liberty, equality and so on, which are the decisive influence in this matter also. It is one of the evils which accompany the benefits of a free state. But we ought patiently to accept the bad with the good. Look about in town and countryside. The journeyman wants to be a master before his time; the shop-boy wants to be a shop-keeper at once; the farmer's sons all want to be farmers, and so they parcel out their father's farm into small patches; the servant-boy follows the trend, giving up his place in order to be his own master. And so they marry whether they have anything to marry on or not. If it goes wrong, they blame the hard times. People today won't readily examine themselves to see the cause of their disappointment and misfortune in their own conduct. It is not easy to see how it will change, but the matter has become so alarming, that if the country is to survive, it would seem necessary that it must. So we can but hope for the best.'

When the people most obviously sympathetic towards the common man's plight speak out in this way, then one knows that the vehement and the passionate, who are usually in the majority, are hardly likely to be restrained in their judgements. Not for them the charitable and loving words that are needed most whenever a serious judgement must be pronounced. Thus whenever poor people start a family prematurely and thoughtlessly, which all too easily can increase the community's burdens and finally recoil upon the rich, so are the minds and voices of the wealthy turned with harshness and scorn upon the poor.

4 But whether it is sympathy and goodwill, or hard feelings and anger that reign in the heart, the general opinion is that the frequency of imprudent marriages amongst the poorer classes is a growing and threatening evil. There is a disquiet prevalent in many minds, as when a river has risen above its usual height and when its rapid current is not only undermining its banks, but is also threatening to flood and wreak havoc far around.

One is immediately reassured when it appears that the menacing river has ceased to rise: better still, when it looks as though the river has even begun to fall, if only by an inch or so.

And I believe that it really has fallen that much, possibly even more.

5 It is exceedingly important that this matter be decided one way or the other. Should it be so that, not only is it often the case, but also that it is becoming more and more common, for poor and simple folk to marry at a young and altogether premature age; that there is a sad absence of cool thinking about a step which is of so great importance, both for the individuals concerned and for the community's well-being, namely the establishment of a family, then we must know it, beyond any possibility of doubt. For then, the sound and healthy forces within the community can combine and conquer such a fundamental evil. If

on the other hand it is the case that the evil has not spread further and is perhaps on the wane, this also ought to be known. The view that the community is dangerously threatened by the rudeness of the masses is well-calculated to arouse the energies of the upper classes. But it is also well-suited to create ill-feeling and give rise to bitterness and discontent on both sides. If one holds, on the other hand, the view that the life of the community is growing rather better, that the increase in enlightenment and morality that is now taking place amongst the upper classes, will little by little seep through to the masses and will then lead and direct their thought and life, so will the men whom Providence has set in such a position that they are able to exercise some influence upon the people and contribute to their advance in knowledge and well-being, undoubtedly work with greater delight and hope. Their work too will bear a richer fruit. Those people who hold this more optimistic point of view, ought least of all, therefore, to remain silent during the frequent discussion of this topic.

6 I turn back to the story about Ole and Karen. When I came to their home I was myself ready to inveigh loudly against these rash marriages. By up-bringing and profession I belong to a circle of people who, almost without exception, counsel extreme care so far as the decision to establish a family is concerned. With my accustomed ideas and views about this matter I was bound to be astounded, indeed dismayed, when, some years ago whilst travelling around the country, I began to learn of the practices and ways of thinking on this matter in other circles. I must in truth say that my judgement too was often sharp and hard. Indeed on the very day that I found my way to the home of Ole and Karen, I had, as often on other occasions, decided to do nothing less than carry out a thorough investigation of each house in this small parish, to see how it went with the people in this regard, expecting to contemplate and examine recklessness and rudeness triumphant. But it struck me that the family of which, on my entry into their beautifully decorated parlour, I had got such a good impression, had begun with one of these 'thoughtless marriages'. Who could be seated comfortably in that well-lit room, where so many things bore witness to the industry, prosperity and virtue of its occupants; who could be seated here and listen to the story of the wooden spoon and the hat, and still maintain a stern look and a harsh judgement? God had strangely blessed them, so that things had gone well from that day to this. But that was not all. He had still more mercifully led and directed them through life, so that 'the folly of youth' little by little had given way to discretion and industry and prudence. That goodness which lay at the heart, little by

little sprouted forth; that goodness which, I am becoming more and more inclined to believe, is at home in the smallest, the rudest and most erring, when they are born and bred of Norwegian women, and reared amongst the common people of Norway. That a change for the better had occurred in Ole and Karen's way of thinking and demeanour was obvious. And what now? Could it not be possible, so I thought, that a similar change for the better had begun amongst the mass of the people? A whole people can in many way be likened to a single person. Is it not possible, therefore, that the people in the days ahead, under the pressure of the times, under the press and hardships such as Ole and Karen in their little world had been forced to experience, would react in the same way as they did? For little by little their eyes had opened wider and they had laid aside some of the giddiness, the recklessness and rudeness, which had once reigned and threatened to strangle the goodness of their innermost heart, their Norwegian sobriety.

7 Once the idea had occurred to me I found later in other houses, and in other districts, more and more that seemed to agree with it. That is how opinions form themselves. One is struck by a glaring example of a disgraceful thoughtlessness, occurring just on that occasion in life which most of all should make one take things seriously, namely marriage, and from then on one easily finds more and more examples that confirm one's growing opinion of a perilous and increasing evil. I am rather lately come to another view. But in order to make my contribution so that a satisfactory conclusion can be reached in this matter, I have assembled just about all the reliable facts that I have found, with reference to this one aspect of the life of the Norwegian people. To present them is the task of this essay.

Surveys of this kind are truly a work of patience, both for those who shall lead the way and for those who would follow. One must work one's way through a mass of figures and calculations, just as if one was trudging along a winding road between lakes and rocks. But I have an idea that at many places along the road we shall have views over little-known, yet interesting territory. I foresee also that at the end of the survey, it will not be possible, for the time being, to come to an absolute certainty about everything related to this problem. For even now one needs different pieces of information, upon which, as if they formed a ladder, we could climb to the top of the high pinnacle, the goal of our journey, and from which we should get a proper view of the conduct and circumstances of the people in the valley below. But with all investigating and enquiry one comes eventually to a point where one must say: 'No, now we must turn back and get some new

material: we must begin at the beginning again and collect new facts.'
The first attempt has not failed, if it arouses such a desire and prompts
to such endurance.

And here I can say that the present essay, like a previous one, now
completed and dealing with mortality in Norway, is to a great extent
written with the desire to awaken interest in this kind of study, and
just at this particular moment in time. For this year a census will be
held in the country, which is the best way, though it takes place only
every ten years, of obtaining the facts that are needed by enquiries
covering this, and other aspects of the condition of the people. And
because the census is a matter for everyone, I have also written in a
style that is not the kind usually used in these so-called statistical
essays. I aim to write so that the ordinary man, whom I know is not
normally accustomed to reading this kind of work, will be able to read
this book without too great difficulty or boredom.

2

The number of marriages in the kingdom

8 It is to the credit of the administration that for a long time the parish priests have been charged, at the end of each year, with the task of counting the number of couples they have married, the number of children they have baptized etc. in the course of the year and then, with reporting these totals to the deans and bishops. Without such an arrangement, our knowledge of the subject matter of this essay would have been nothing more than a series of loose impressions which, by no amount of scrutiny, could produce a satisfactory conclusion.

It was as early as the year 1735 that such annual counts were ordered and begun. During the last century, however, the matter was not discharged with the carefulness that was desired, nor were the returns regularly printed and so preserved from destruction. But from 1801 until 1850 reliable returns have been printed each year.[1] The

---

[1] I should here explain that the manuscript and printed tables, together with the other writings from which I have derived material for this present essay, are the same as those used for the already-mentioned *Om Dødeligheden i Norge (On Mortality in Norway)*, Christiania, 1855. I have discussed these primary sources on pp. 14 and 195 of that essay.

For those who might want to discover whether or not I have used these primary sources correctly, I should point out the following:

I have been forced to make some changes in the totals of marriages, births etc. for the kingdom as a whole and for the dioceses in the year 1838, as well as for the Christiania and Christiansand Dioceses in the six years 1845–50. On this I refer to the aforementioned essay (see footnote on p. 20 and app. 2).

Statistiske Tabeller for Kongeriget Norge 4de Raekke (Statistical Tables for the Kingdom of Norway 4th series), Christiania, 1839, is a most important collection of statistics for the present essay. It has therefore been all the more necessary to correct a mistake which occurs in it. The work contains details of marriages, births and deaths in the kingdom and dioceses year by year from 1801 to 1835. But in those for the year 1801, the totals for the Tromsø Diocese are counted twice, since firstly they are added to those for the Throndhjem Diocese, which by that means has got too large a total, and then in the next place are given for the Tromsø Diocese. The mistake is occasioned by the fact that, at that time, these two dioceses were joined together. It is corrected in this way: one subtracts the totals given for the Tromsø Diocese from those of the Throndhjem Diocese and the kingdom as a whole. I had long entertained a suspicion that this was the case, but I was first certain of it when, after the whole of this essay had been

present time is a rather inviting one, from the point of view of making ourselves more closely acquainted with the matters with which these returns deal. We can, as it were, pause at that great milestone, the half-century, and cast a searching glance at the past fifty years with all its various changes of fortune.

9 The total number of marriages in our country in the fifty years from 1801 to 1850 was 416,667. A significant total! Almost all of us find in this figure the start of our own or our parents' marriage. It embraces the public official and the ordinary citizen, the farmer, the fisherman and the day labourer, the Lapp and the Norwegian, the highest and the lowest, the educated and the illiterate. This total comprises an even greater sum of Holy vows, of love and joy, of cold and selfish calculation, of base thoughtlessness and fatal passion; an immeasurable sum of heavenly promise, of the Lord's blessing as well as the Lord's judgement. The size of the total is well suited to remind us of the familiar expression that, in the blessings of married life, in the love and harmony, joy and peace of the family, lies the nation's fortune and strength. There must be many a man in Norway, for whom the word 'Fatherland' or 'Patriotism' is almost a foreign term, strange and long-winded. He has heard its sound, possibly tried to pronounce it himself, on occasion, but never, perhaps, apprehended its meaning or tasted its sweetness. But it is good that he has grown up in a happy home, that he has been born and reared by pious parents, in a household where love has earned his gratitude, where industriousness and enterprise have planted in his soul a desire for order and for action, where harmony and a firm will have sown a feeling for morality in his breast, a respect for the good and an obedience to the right. So he is a good citizen, firstly in his home, in his neighbourhood, his parish; and then too in his Fatherland, even if the word itself is too great for his understanding to grasp. There is a particular reason why we should dwell with pleasure upon the fact that the Lord blessed domestic life as the foundation of a nation's fortune. For when we normally speak about a nation, we think about its past and its present, about its achievements and its honours. So that it is mostly about men that we think. It is therefore extremely rare that an individual woman stands out from the rest of her sex, to the extent that she is seen to exercise some particularly noteworthy influence upon the nation as a whole. But

completed, I quite accidentally unearthed, in the Statistical Bureau's Archives, the original of the bishop's list. Since there was now no doubt about the matter, I was compelled to correct all the totals and calculations in which the details printed in the tables for 1801 had been used. [For further comments and revised totals see Drake, *Population and Society* – Ed.]

if we look upon the nation as a collection of families we realize immediately that here it is the woman who embellishes life, who, in her
husband nourishes, and in her sons awakens, that spirit of order and
peace and mildness, in which the powers that be find their real strength.

   10 But we must proceed and see what variations have occurred in
the number of marriages at different times during the last half century.
I have therefore divided up the total and given the number of marriages
in each individual year (Table 1). If we now glance at the long series
of numbers, two things in particular meet the eye. On the one hand it
is soon apparent that the totals for the later years are on the whole
greater than those for the earlier; and on the other hand, as the figures
are constantly rising and falling from year to year, it is difficult to grasp
any trend in the movement.

Table 1. *Annual totals of marriages in Norway, 1801–54*

Year	Total	Year	Total	Year	Total	Year	Total
1801	6,089	1816	9,427	1831	8,190	1846	11,152
1802	6,742	1817	8,010	1832	7,839	1847	9,890
1803	6,790	1818	7,713	1833	8,548	1848	10,187
1804	7,069	1819	7,721	1834	8,872	1849	10,629
1805	7,227	1820	8,712	1835	8,784	1850	10,648
1806	7,283	1821	8,895	1836	8,424	1851	10,575
1807	6,331	1822	8,949	1837	8,123	1852	10,179
1808	5,305	1823	8,841	1838	7,584	1853	11,257
1809	5,370	1824	8,376	1839	7,949	1854	12,479
1810	7,100	1825	9,020	1840	8,601		
1811	7,854	1826	8,805	1841	9,595		
1812	7,850	1827	8,087	1842	9,962		
1813	6,453	1828	8,358	1843	10,173		
1814	5,801	1829	8,639	1844	10,290		
1815	9,171	1830	8,669	1845	10,570		

   11 For the latter reason I have produced a shorter series giving the
number of marriages for each five years (Table 2).

   These totals provide an easy and convenient summary. We see
immediately that there are great differences in the different periods,
but we also get the impression that these differences are not merely
accidental. There is a certain smoothness and regularity in the passage
from the higher to the lower totals and vice-versa. We can observe a
definite trend in the movement.

   This trend is as follows: the number of marriages falls from the first
to the second five-year period. Then it rises until the period 1821–25,
where the number of marriages reaches its first high point. The number

Table 2. *Five-yearly totals of*
marriages in Norway, 1801–50

Years	Total
1801–05	33,917
1806–10	31,389
1811–15	37,129
1816–20	41,583
1821–25	44,081
1826–30	42,558
1831–35	42,233
1836–40	40,681
1841–45	50,590
1846–50	52,506
Total	416,667

then falls, again smoothly, for three five-year periods though it does not sink as low as it did on the other side of the high point. But in the years 1841–45 it rises again suddenly and sharply, even higher than it did at the previous high point, and in the ensuing period it rises even further. The characteristic of this last rise is its suddenness, as we can see from Table 1. Up to and including the year 1840 the totals remain low. Then suddenly in 1841, they rise higher than in any preceding year and remain so, or rise to an even greater height in each of the following years.

12. This rise and fall can be shown even more clearly. There are just ten five-year periods between 1801 and 1850. If the size of the population and all else had been absolutely identical in each of these five-year periods, then the overall number of marriages would have been the same. In each period, there would have been just 10 per cent of the grand total of 416,667; in other words 41,666$\frac{7}{10}$. This latter total we can call the average. But in real life the situation has been otherwise. The actual totals rise and fall and therefore are sometimes over and sometimes under this average figure. This rise and fall, or these changes, we can regard as deviations from the average.

But the average total (or mean figure) of 41,666$\frac{7}{10}$ is too complex for us, composed as it is of thousands, hundreds, tens, units and a fraction. It is both difficult to manipulate and to remember. When we are dealing with the relationship between the five-year periods it is more convenient if we calculate a simpler total. Instead of the actual average of 41,666$\frac{7}{10}$ I will take it to be 1,000. The totals for the different five-year periods must be altered accordingly, so that the overall position remains unchanged. Thus, for example, for the five years 1846–50, I must substitute the figure 1,260 for the actual figure of 52,506.

In this particular five-year period the number of marriages deviates from the average number as 1,260 deviates from 1,000. I can also express this in another way, since for each 1,000 marriages that, according to the average total, there should have been, there were 260 more. But 260 in each 1,000 is the same as 26 in each 100, or to use another expression, 26 per cent. I can therefore say that the number of marriages in this particular five-year period was 26 per cent above the average.

With this prefatory note I can now present the whole series in the same way (Table 3).

Table 3. *Five-yearly totals of marriages as a percentage of the mean number of marriages in Norway, 1801–50*

Years	On an average of 1,000 the number would be:	The percentage above (+) or below (−) the average
1801–05	814	−18.6
1806–10	753	−24.7
1811–15	891	−10.9
1816–20	998	−0.2
1821–25	1,058	+5.8
1826–30	1,021	+2.1
1831–35	1,014	+1.4
1836–40	976	−2.4
1841–45	1,215	+21.5
1846–50	1,260	+26.0
Average	1,000	0.0

13 If we now look again at the numerical series we see that the whole fifty years divides into three distinct sections:

1. The first two five-year periods when the number of marriages is about 20 per cent under the average. To this section is joined the years 1811–15, which period acts as a sort of link to the next section.
2. The five-year periods from 1816 to 40 when the number of marriages keeps close to the average number, or only rises or falls by some few per cent.
3. The last two five years of the half-century (as well as the five years 1851–55, see Table 1), where the number of marriages is more than 20 per cent above the average.

14 The phenomenon, characterized by the words 'rise and fall' or 'over and under' may be shown more clearly in a diagram by a winding line. I have tried to draw this and so beg the reader to cast an eye at Figure 1.

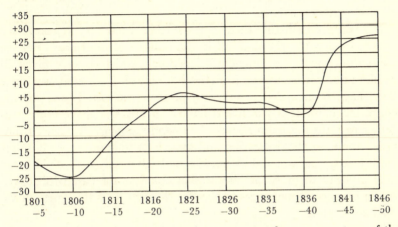

Figure 1. Five-yearly totals of marriages, expressed as a percentage of the mean number of marriages 1801–50, in Norway.

The somewhat long rectangular space is divided from left to right by ten upright lines. These correspond to the ten five-year periods. The thick straight line which goes through the middle of the figure from left to right, shows us how the diagram would have appeared if the number of marriages had been identical in each of the five-year periods, that is, if they had been neither over nor under the average. The winding line on the other hand shows us how the actual number of marriages in each of the five-year periods deviates from the average. When the actual total is less than the average total, the winding line sinks under the middle line. On the other hand it rises above it when the total is greater. This rise and fall corresponds to the previously calculated percentages, as is indicated by the upright line on the extreme left.

With such a graph we could also represent the rise and fall of the water in a river. One must measure the water-level at different times of the year; one must then calculate how much the water-level in the spring and autumn stood above, and how much in the winter it dropped below the average, and the percentage differences can then be marked out on the paper.

An annual experience of many years standing has taught us what it is that brings about such a rise and fall in a river. When for example we see the water rising, we conclude that thawing weather has melted the snow in the mountains. If we are in the mountains and can observe the warm sun melting the snow then we foresee that the river will rise. In the same manner we presume that the rise and fall in the number of marriages is something which also has its causes and that it should be possible to discover these.

But before considering these causes further, I must try to answer the question – has the rise and fall in the number of marriages been the same throughout the kingdom? The totals which I have given in Tables 1 and 2 are made up from those of each of the five dioceses, since these have been added together to produce the grand total for the entire kingdom. It is like five tributary streams that have flowed together to form the main stream. Frequently amongst five such tributaries, some are flooded earlier and some later than others, or to put it more briefly, the water does not rise and fall evenly and at the same time in all of them. Something similar could be the case with regard to the number of marriages in the five dioceses. It is this question we shall now resolve.

3

The number of marriages in the five dioceses

15 First of all I give the number of marriages in each five-year period in the same way as I did for the entire kingdom in Table 2. We see immediately that in the Christiania Diocese the total number of marriages is always much greater than in the other dioceses, whilst in the Tromsø Diocese it is always smaller. This is due to the fact that the population in the former is so great compared to what it is in the other dioceses, whilst in the latter it is so small. But it is not the actual number of marriages that concerns us here. What we asked at the end of the previous chapter was whether the number of marriages rises and falls at approximately the same rate and time in each of the five dioceses. This we can ascertain from Table 4.

Table 4. *Five-yearly totals of marriages in the dioceses of Norway, 1801–50*

Years	Christiania	Christiansand	Bergen	Throndhjem	Tromsø
1801–05	14,181	5,223	6,223	5,057	3,223
1806–10	13,269	4,742	5,612	4,480	3,286
1811–15	17,077	5,863	6,461	4,985	2,809
1816–20	18,300	6,259	7,300	6,294	3,430
1821–25	19,527	6,742	7,315	6,774	3,723
1826–30	17,506	6,634	7,621	6,977	3,820
1831–35	17,210	6,897	7,688	6,743	3,695
1836–40	16,573	7,065	7,206	6,122	3,715
1841–45	21,546	8,213	8,665	7,641	4,525
1846–50	22,958	8,253	9,011	7,336	4,948
Total	178,091	65,891	73,102	62,409	37,174

16 To compare the many totals in the five series is awkward. I have, therefore, made a calculation which makes it easier to see the relationship between the different five-year periods. This was done in just the same way as I explained earlier in the case of Table 3. The result of this calculation is to be found in Table 5.

Table 5. *Five-yearly totals of marriages in the dioceses of Norway per 1,000 of the mean number of marriages in each, 1801–50**

Years	Christiania	Christiansand	Bergen	Throndhjem	Tromsø
1801–05	797	793	851	810	867
1806–10	745	720	768	718	884
1811–15	955	890	884	799	756
1816–20	1,028	950	998	1,009	923
1821–25	1,096	1,023	1,001	1,085	1,002
1826–30	983	1,007	1,043	1,118	1,027
1831–35	966	1,047	1,052	1,080	994
1836–40	931	1,072	986	981	999
1841–45	1,210	1,246	1,185	1,224	1,217
1846–50	1,289	1,252	1,232	1,176	1,331
Average	1,000	1,000	1,000	1,000	1,000

* As we have said, one should note in this Table 5, not whether the number of marriages in the one diocese is greater or smaller than in another, but whether the number rises or falls at anything like the same rate and at the same time in each. The large number of marriages in the Christiania Diocese rose from the years 1836–40 to the years 1841–45 to the extent that the number 931 rises to 1,210; the small number of marriages in the Tromsø Diocese rose in the same period to the extent that 999 rises to 1,217. In both dioceses therefore, the rise was marked, and it is this which we intend to show here.

Now it is fairly easy to compare the rise and fall in the five dioceses. We can summarize the changes as follows.

1. The number of marriages is, in general, smaller in the second five-year period than in the first. The only exception is the Tromsø Diocese, where the reverse is the case. But the difference is not great.

2. In the third five-year period, 1811–15, the total begins to rise markedly in the Christiania Diocese, less so in Christiansand and Bergen and even less in the Throndhjem Diocese. In the Tromsø Diocese it actually falls. It looks then as if the fall, mentioned in the previous paragraph, was now taking place in the Tromsø Diocese, i.e. five years later than elsewhere.

3. From 1816–20, up to and including 1836–40, that is, for 25 years, there is first a rise and then a fall in four of the dioceses. The diocese which provides the exception is Christiansand. Here a slight rise continues up to and including the period 1836–40.

4. In 1841–45 the totals rise very markedly in all five dioceses, and maintain the same high level or rise even further in 1846–50.

5. Essentially the figures in each of the five dioceses move in the same direction throughout the period and so are in accord with those presented earlier for the kingdom as a whole.

17 A clearer idea of the whole matter is obtained if we note by how much the number of marriages in each five-year period deviates in percentage terms from the average (see Table 6). We did this previously for the kingdom as a whole in Table 3.

Table 6. *By how many per cent the number of marriages, in each five-year period, is above or below the mean, in each of the dioceses of Norway, 1801–50*

Years	Christiania	Christiansand	Bergen	Throndhjem	Tromsø
1801–05	−20.3	−20.7	−14.9	−19.0	−13.3
1806–10	−25.5	−28.0	−23.2	−28.2	−11.6
1811–15	−4.5	−11.0	−11.6	−20.1	−24.4
1816–20	+2.8	−5.9	−0.2	+0.9	−7.7
1821–25	+9.6	+2.3	+0.1	+8.5	+0.2
1826–30	−1.7	+0.7	+4.3	+11.8	+2.7
1831–35	−3.4	+4.7	+5.2	+8.0	−0.6
1836–40	−6.9	+7.2	−1.4	−1.4	−0.1
1841–45	+21.0	+24.6	+18.5	+22.4	+21.7
1846–50	+28.9	+25.2	+23.2	+17.6	+33.1

Earlier, in paragraph 13, it was shown that, as far as the total number of marriages was concerned, the 10 five-year periods could be broken up into three groups. These cover the years 1801–15, 1816–40 and 1841–50. It is fairly obvious that the same period grouping can be applied to each of the five dioceses. The most noticeable exception to this is to be found in the years 1811–15. During these years the Christiania Diocese appears to be the first to move into the second of the three periods, the Christiansand and Bergen Dioceses represent a transitional state between the first and second period, whilst the two northerly dioceses still remain within the first period.

The similarity between the dioceses is quite remarkable in two ways. First, the rise and fall in the number of marriages occurs more or less at the same time and, secondly, the magnitude of the changes is roughly equal in each of the five dioceses.

18 In order to bring out this remarkable similarity I have drawn a graph (Figure 2) like the one I did for the kingdom as a whole (Figure 1). The five winding lines, representing the five dioceses, indicate the rise and fall in the marriage totals. Line 1 represents the Christiania Diocese; line 2 the Christiansand Diocese; lines 3, 4, and 5, the Bergen, Throndhjem and Tromsø Dioceses respectively. The more the lines run side by side, the greater the agreement between the dioceses. On the whole one sees that they do this quite strikingly.

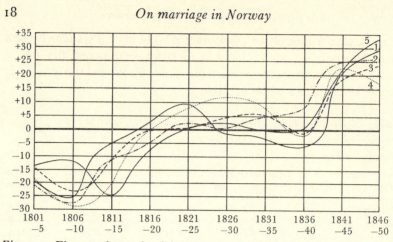

Figure 2. Five-yearly totals of marriages, expressed as a percentage of the mean number of marriages 1801–50, in each of the dioceses of Norway.

19 After what we have now seen regarding the kingdom as a whole and its major sub-divisions, one might presume that the rule that applies to them, regarding the increase and decrease of the number of marriages at certain times, will also apply to the various smaller districts of the country. However, it is possible to imagine that there could be deviations from the rule. It would not, therefore, surprise us to find that the situation is different in, for example, the outer districts of the Christiania Diocese as against the upland areas. It is, therefore worthwhile investigating this more closely by comparing the number of marriages in the deaneries of Laurvik, Jarlsberg, Hedemarken and Gudbrandsdalen (Tables 7 and 8).

Table 7. *Five-yearly totals of marriages in the deaneries of Laurvik, Jarlsberg, Hedemarken and Gudbrandsdalen, 1801–50*

Years	Laurvik	Jarlsberg	Hedemarken	Gudbrands-dalen
1801–05	639	984	847	966
1806–10	682	913	906	1,002
1811–15	907	1,086	1,146	1,088
1816–20	816	1,147	1,189	1,389
1821–25	875	1,298	1,118	1,504
1826–30	689	1,182	1,042	1,403
1831–35	795	1,170	1,028	1,239
1836–40	811	1,179	870	954
1841–45	947	1,353	1,225	1,549
1846–50	1,040	1,483	1,353	1,561
Total	8,201	11,795	10,724	12,655

Table 8. *Five-yearly totals of marriages in the deaneries of Laurvik, Jarlsberg, Hedemarken and Gudbrandsdalen, per 1,000 of the mean number of marriages in each, 1801–50*

Years	Laurvik	Jarlsberg	Hedemarken	Gudbrands-dalen
1801–05	779	834	790	763
1806–10	832	774	845	792
1811–15	1,106	921	1,069	860
1816–20	995	973	1,109	1,098
1821–25	1,067	1,100	1,042	1,188
1826–30	840	1,002	971	1,109
1831–35	969	992	959	979
1836–40	989	1,000	811	754
1841–45	1,155	1,147	1,142	1,224
1846–50	1,268	1,257	1,262	1,233
Average	1,000	1,000	1,000	1,000

When we look at the figures, particularly at those in Table 8, we do indeed find less regularity and uniformity than in the corresponding totals for the kingdom and for the Christiania Diocese (See Tables 3 and 5). But it is in the main still fairly easy to see a resemblance between them: small totals for the first two five-year periods, an increase to around the year 1825, a falling off towards 1840 and from there a rise, and a marked rise at that.

20 We can test this rule on some individual parishes, for example the three northernmost ones in the Gudbrandsdalen Deanery. The totals for these are to be found in Tables 9 and 10. Here the regularity is even less apparent than in the totals for the deaneries. A marked

Table 9. *Five-yearly totals of marriages in the parishes of Lom, Vaage and Lesje, 1801–50*

Years	Lom	Vaage	Lesje
1801–05	93	117	119
1806–10	124	122	142
1811–15	160	134	134
1816–20	152	194	184
1821–25	183	179	231
1826–30	120	187	230
1831–35	131	140	172
1836–40	103	101	126
1841–45	197	216	193
1846–50	170	213	186
Total	1,433	1,603	1,717

Table 10. *Five-yearly totals of marriages in the parishes of Lom, Vaage and Lesje as a percentage of the mean number of marriages in each, 1801–50*

Years	Lom	Vaage	Lesje
1801–05	65	73	69
1806–10	86	76	83
1811–15	112	84	78
1816–20	106	121	107
1821–25	128	112	135
1826–30	84	117	134
1831–35	91	87	100
1836–40	72	63	73
1841–45	137	134	113
1846–50	119	133	108
Average	100	100	100

deviation from the usual rule is that in the years 1841–45, as well as in the years 1846–50, the totals for Lesje Parish are not as great as they were around 1825.[1] Nevertheless, there is still an unmistakable accord between them and the Gudbrandsdalen Deanery, the Christiania Diocese and the kingdom as a whole. In each individual parish we find small totals in the first two or three five-year periods, then a considerable rise to 1825 or 1830, a fall to 1840, and then another rise.

It was not by accident that I chose the parishes of Lom and Vaage for my examples. In 1851 I had travelled through a great deal of Smaalenene, Hedemarken, Gudbrandsdalen and Østerdalen, with the intention of acquiring information, principally about the way of life of the lower classes. On this long journey I had seen and heard a lot that was new to me but had not learned much very thoroughly. The following year I picked out a single parish so that I might devote greater attention to a smaller sphere and so get actual illustrations of the circumstances and customs of the people. My choice fell upon Lom. Since I was just then eager to learn of the much discussed topic of reckless marriages, something about which I was greatly concerned personally, I took great pains to find out what marriage conditions were like. I began in the following way. From the parish registers I made a list of the names of the couples who had married in the previous five years. I then went out into the parish in order to enquire into the earlier and present circumstances of these people; their economic

[1] From Gudbrandsdalen in general, and from Lesje Parish in particular, there was in this later period a heavy emigration of young people; this is the reason why the number of marriages from 1841 onwards did not rise as much as it otherwise would have done.

state, their ways of thought, their customs. By preference, I sought out the families themselves in their own homes and conversed directly with the people concerned. I asked my questions in a straightforward manner and I must commend the people highly for the direct and trusting way in which, for the most part, I was answered. But I did not find all those directly concerned at home, or their houses lay so far off that I did not have the time to seek them out. So I asked about them at the houses of reliable people in the neighbourhood. In this way I got a great many illustrations of actual conditions in the parish and noted down many views on the matter. Within the parish I was, in so far as the short space of a couple of months and the pressure of other work would allow, initiated into the family circumstances and prevailing habits regarding this matter. The question was – did the talk of reckless marriages apply to this parish? Were reckless marriages here more frequent in recent times than formerly, or were they more frequent here than in other parishes in the country? These questions were as yet by no means answered, so I went back to the parsonage and made another search through the parish registers. I totalled the number of marriages year by year from 1736, that being as far back as the register went, until the present day. Then I went out once again and made a point of conversing with the old people, in order to ascertain if, over time, changes had taken place in employment, wealth, ways of thought and customs, which could have brought about the fact that the number of marriages was sometimes greater, sometimes smaller, but always rising and falling. On this occasion, as in other places, I was bound to note that although the Norwegian farmer is remarkably conversant with present conditions in his parish, indeed almost within each and every house, his knowledge is very imperfect and confused about the conditions and events of earlier times. However, I was lucky enough to gather a considerable amount of information, sometimes here, sometimes there, relative to this matter. And after putting these pieces of information together, after comparing the old with the new, after examining them in the light of the totals taken from the registers, after drawing up many more lists from the registers (of legitimate and illegitimate births, as well as of deaths) after again and again gazing at the totals and meditating upon them, lo and behold it happened! Little by little there formed in my mind a view of the matter, and one that was by no means the same as that I had brought with me to the parish. During an admittedly much shorter stay in the neighbouring parish of Vaage, where I also sought out the people in their own homes and drew up long lists from the parish registers, this same view was confirmed.

What I had learned here I carried with me on other journeys throughout the country, and especially in 1853 through much of the dioceses of Christiansand and Bergen. My interpretation of the matter was further strengthened by such experiences as those I spoke of in the opening chapter.

In 1854, I went again to Lom and Vaage, and at the same place where the idea, so to speak, was born, I repeated the entire exercise as far as that was possible, in order to reassure myself that I had made no mistakes in the matter. Here in Christiania where in part handwritten and in part printed tables have been compiled from the parish registers of the entire kingdom, I continued to examine the Gudbrandsdalen and Hedemarken deaneries, the Christiania Diocese and the kingdom as a whole. Everywhere I found that same rising and falling in the number of marriages that I had first discovered in the Lom and Vaage parishes. The more wide-ranging my investigation, the more I felt that the view formed in Lom was the answer. In this and the previous chapter, I have shown the links between the various pieces of evidence that strengthened me in my opinion. The opinion itself will be discussed in the following chapters.[2]

21 At the end of the last chapter I compared the rise and fall of the number of marriages to the rise and fall of the water in a river. Likewise, the comparison continues here. The totals for the kingdom are arrived at by adding together the totals for the five dioceses, in much the same way as a main stream is formed by the running together of many tributaries. The symbol of the main stream and the tributaries represents the relationship between the kingdom and the dioceses, as the small streams and brooks correspond to the deaneries and parishes. The rise and fall of a river always shows itself more regularly and

[2] It is the custom for writers to acknowledge with gratitude the names of the men who have especially encouraged and assisted them in their enquiries. I must therefore, with thanks, name that worthy and intelligent farmer, Erik Pedersen Rusten of Baeverdalen in Lom. I came as a complete stranger to this man's house, and the object of my stay in the parish was unknown to him. But he was so able to familiarize himself with my interests that he patiently listened to all my questions and brought together all his memories and experiences concerning the matter, in a conversation that lasted from morning till night for an entire eight days. I was therefore very sorry to learn, on my second visit, that this man was away, seeking medical assistance for a critical eye complaint. However, I again found men who both could and would engage in long and valuable conversations with me; especially that sharp-witted farmer Ole Gudbrandson Kvaale of Baerdalen, and the thoughtful crofter John Jonson Jons-Gjaerdet of Gjøingslien under Nordherred's-Marken. It was during these conversations that I conceived the idea of this book. To write it is for me the same as to talk afresh with these and other men, with whom, in conversation on these and other matters, I spent many very happy hours.

smoothly in its mainstream, much less so, on the other hand, in the small brooks where so many tiny unsettling factors are at work. In the same way, the rise and fall in the totals of marriages is most regular in the case of the kingdom as a whole, least so in the case of the parishes. Nevertheless, we do find, for the most part, a similarity between the totals for the kingdom and those for the parishes and we conclude from this that whilst in the single parish there are many accidental, incalculable, minor disturbing elements at work, there must also be one or more deeply embedded reasons, that have resulted in the number of marriages rising and falling at more or less the same time in different places. It is to this that I would now like to draw attention.

4

On the reasons for the rising and falling number of marriages in the kingdom

22 As there is such a remarkable regularity in this rise and fall, and as the causes of this are understood to have been so general and so marked, affecting all the kingdom, it ought to be possible to discover what they are. What then are these causes? Is it unusually good and fruitful seasons, a booming commerce and business that, at certain times, have allowed more people than usual to acquire the means of establishing a family and of standing on their own two feet? Is it that, at other times, dearth, bad years and stoppages in trade, have, to a great extent, reduced people's chances of obtaining a livelihood and so compelled them to put off getting married? Or perhaps the reasons lie not so much outside people but within them? Is it perhaps the case that at certain times, over a period of ten years or so, thoughtlessness reigns leading many people to give way to their natural impulses and to marry without any further thought for their daily bread and all the other growing needs of a family? Is it true that at other times the contrary has occurred, a certain timorousness of spirit has developed? Or perhaps many have set less value on the blessings of marriage and the comforts of married life than they should?

One will thus understand that the investigator who goes out to find the reason, or the different reasons, for the variation in the number of marriages during a particular period, must also make a contribution to our understanding of the fortunes and habits of the people.

23 First, we should hear what some well-informed men have said on the matter. It is true that, for the most part, these men have talked about the increase of population in general. But when this rests essentially upon the increase in the number of marriages, or, in other words, upon the number of children born, and on the lessening of mortality amongst these, so their remarks do apply to a great extent to the matter we have before us. However, in order to be able to understand their contributions, which I shall come to in a moment, I first of all give the size of the population as recorded at the various censuses and its increase from one time to another (Table 11).

(The last column in the table is designed to show that if the population continued to increase at the same rate, as for example from 1825 to 1835, then it would have doubled in the course of $54\frac{1}{2}$ years.)

Table 11. *The growth of population in Norway, 1769–1845*

Year	Total	Increase from the one census to the next	Number of years between censuses	Yearly increase calculated as %	Time needed for population to double at stated rate of increase
1769	723,141*				
1801, 1 Feb.	883,038	159,897	$31\frac{11}{24}$	0.63	109 yrs
1815, 30 Apr.	885,431	2,393	$14\frac{1}{4}$	—	—
1825, 27 Nov.	1,051,318	165,887	$10\frac{7}{12}$	1.7	43
1835, 29 Nov.	1,194,827	143,509	10	1.3	$54\frac{1}{2}$
1845, 31 Dec.	1,328,471	133,644	$10\frac{1}{12}$	1.1	$63\frac{1}{3}$

* The totals up to 1835 are taken from Schweigaard's *Statistik*. On the 1769 census, which can be more correctly put at 748,000, see *sml. Norsk Tidsskr. f. Vid. og Litt.* 1848, p. 398.

Professor Holst has written a painstaking essay *Om Folketaellingen i Norge i Aaret 1825 (On the Census of Norway in the year 1825)*.[1] Here he speaks first of all about the period between the censuses of 1801 and 1815, when the increase in population was almost nil. 'But the last half (1807–14) of this period', he writes, 'was full of reasons that must not only have checked the increase of population but even brought about its decline. At the outbreak of war businesses stopped and unaccustomed obstacles were thrown in the way of the import of the necessary quantity of corn and other foodstuffs. And although the cultivation of corn and potatoes was, in these five years and in certain districts of the kingdom, increased considerably, the yield was not great enough to overcome an annual shortfall of several hundred thousands of bushels. Already this alone caused a considerable dearth which increased, in particular in the summer of 1812, throughout almost the entire country as a result of a general crop failure or a poor harvest of both corn and hay. As a result many farmers were compelled to limit considerably the stock on their farms. For want of sound and nutritious food, people were compelled to seize upon straw, *Rumex crispus, Anagallis, Brassica oleracea* and *rapa, Lichen islandicus* and *rangiferinus, Polypodium filix mas*, the bark of *Betula alba*, dry fish and fishbones made into

[1] In *Budstikken*, 1827, nos. 80–9.

flour etc. Eating these caused fatal diseases, in particular, dysentery and putrid fever, mostly in the years 1808, 1809, 1812 and 1813. Furthermore these sicknesses caused much greater ravages since the cause, namely want, could not be removed, nor could doctors and medicines be obtained everywhere. Besides all this a number were carried off by smallpox etc. in the years 1805, 1810 and 1811.'

On the other hand the increase in population between the censuses of 1815 and 1825, was so great (see Table 11) that, as the writer points out, not until that time could it be matched anywhere in Europe. 'As to the reasons for this marked increase', so the Professor continues, 'it seems the following must be considered pre-eminent. Experience shows that organic activity, when it wakes to a new life after a period of rest, usually demonstrates an increased vigour. Consonant with this experience one can therefore perhaps declare that Norway's population, after stagnating for many unfortunate years at the beginning of this decade, began to rise and especially so in those parts of the kingdom which, in the previous period, had suffered most loss or which had increased least. Since 1814, the country has enjoyed a constant peace under which, not only have old businesses revived, but many new ones opened. The nation has become better educated, partly by the founding of the university and of many grammar schools and partly by the considerable improvement in the parish schools. In medicine there have also been various important improvements, with many medical posts established. Vaccination, though no doubt introduced and decreed in an earlier period, has been adopted more widely than formerly, particularly since the smallpox epidemics in Smaalenene, Akershus, Buskerud, Jarlsberg, Laurvik and Bratsberg in the years 1819 and 1820. In addition to this, although epidemics, both of smallpox and other diseases, have broken out almost annually here and there, for the most part they have been very mild and in all of them mortality has been very low. The earth's produce has been plentiful and good in most years and neither a general crop failure nor a bad harvest has occurred for some years. Thus the nation has been able to furnish itself with an adequate amount of good and wholesome food usually at very low prices.' In conclusion the writer draws one's attention to the fact that the number of allodial disputes at law in this period has been especially small. Ordinarily these have contributed to the neglect of agriculture, or even vandalism and the destruction of woods, which again were bound to be detrimental to population growth.

Professor Holst had himself, as a man of mature years, lived through and observed that most important period in Norway's history, just before and after 1814; a period which, for the majority of people living today, is but a vague memory. We must, therefore, be indebted to him for his writings on population conditions in those years.

24 In the year 1840 Professor Schweigaard published his *Norges Statistik* (*Norway's Statistics*), in which the last chapter dealt with population. The Professor had at his disposal the figures from the censuses up to and including 1835 together with the yearly totals of births, marriages and deaths up to the same year.

Schweigaard speaks firstly of the sudden halt in population growth between 1801 and 1815. Essentially he explains it in the same way as Holst, namely as a result of war conditions between 1807 and 1814. 'It is notable however', he adds, 'that the increase in population was very slight also in the particularly profitable years 1801–07. The chief reason for this was the crop failures at the beginning of the century.'

'In the years 1816–1825', so the writer goes on, 'the population of the kingdom increased so fast that one cannot easily find the like of it in any other European country. That the size of the population in that period increased so markedly, despite the fact that, taken on the whole, the kingdom's economic circumstances were not so good,[2] is only a repetition of that same phenomenon that shows itself everywhere in population movements. At the cessation of the suffering which has violently retarded it, the population doubles its efforts and so fills up the gap brought about during the previous period.' This view the author supports by pointing out how the increase in 1815–25, for the most part, had been greatest in those districts of the kingdom where in the years 1801–15 the reduction had been the greatest. 'Among the new reasons for the growth of population, the spread in the cultivation of the potato stands uppermost. The cultivation of this plant has not only increased the population, but also made the peril of famine less threatening.'[3]

'In the period 1826–35, the condition of the common people was, taken on the whole, good, and better than in the previous decade. But the greater part of the deficiency in the population was already made good, which is why we find that the increase is not at the same rate as

---

[2] We ought to note the fact that this last sentence gives another, but without doubt more correct, idea of the economic conditions in the country than that we got from Professor Holst's description.

[3] Regarding this last comment, it ought to be remembered that it was written before the potato blight was known or had become dangerous.

in the years 1816–25.[4] The census, the next time it is held, will without doubt show a proportionately smaller increase than in the former years.'

In later chapters it will be seen that in some matters I agree and in others disagree with Schweigaard's interpretation of the so-called population movements. But for now I shall give some views of writers concerned with the years from 1835 onwards, i.e. the period which most of my readers will have lived to see and ponder over.

25 With regard to the five years 1836–40, we have a statement of that well-known statistician, the late Judge Kraft. Kraft wrote the very interesting introduction to the official *Beretning om Rigets Økonomiske Tilstand (Report on the Kingdom's Economic Situation)* for the aforementioned years. After pointing out that the population had grown less in this five-year period than in the preceding one, he states, 'this less fortunate situation in the last quinquennium is caused in part by greater mortality, but in part it must also be attributed to the smaller number of births, as the number of people getting married was also less in this period.[5] The cause of this must be sought in the bad harvests of 1836, 1837 and 1838. The situation was particularly severe in districts of the Akershus Diocese together with a greater part of the Throndhjem Diocese and the northern areas. Bad seasons, together with business stoppages, brought about unemployment and migration. How important this was as regards the number of new marriages and the increase in population as a whole can be seen when we note that in the unhappy war years of 1813 and 1814 the number of people getting married was respectively: 6,453 and 5,801. In 1815 the number rose to 9,171 and in 1816 to 9,427. Similar results were produced by the war years 1808 and 1809.'

According to this view the marked increase in the number of marriages for the period 1841–45 (Table 2) must be explained by the good years and favourable conditions. And in much the same way is the matter also explained by the official (Department of the Interior) report for the five years 1846–50. Here it is said that 'the rising rate of population increase in the five years 1841–45, as against the previous five years, has decreased somewhat in the last quinquennium,[6] a result easily explained when it is recalled that, whilst in the first five years (1841–45) times were very good, in the period in question (1846–50)

---

[4] This decline in the number of marriages after 1825 can be seen in my Table 2.
[5] See my Table 2.
[6] But look at my Table 2, which shows a marked increase 1841–45, but a much weaker one in 1846–50.

several events occurred which militated against an increase in population. These were: dearth throughout the entire kingdom in 1847;[7] crop failures in several years in the northern part of the country; and unfortunate market conditions for several industries in part of the period as a result of the events of 1848' (the French Revolution).

26 If we were to explain the marked rise and fall in the number of marriages, as presented in Table 2, according to the interpretation which is substantially the same for all the named writers, we would put it as follows:

1801–05, 1806–10, 1811–15:
A small number of marriages resulting from crop failures in the early years of the century and still more from the disruption caused by war in the period 1807–14.

1816–20, 1821–25:
A marked increase in the number of marriages and, on the whole, an unusually large increase in population, caused by the mercurial rise in the people's vital power after the cessation of the suffering of the previous years.

1826–30, 1831–35:
A decreasing number of marriages in spite of the fact that economic conditions were, for the most part, better than in the previous years. But now the great gap was filled. That need for a more numerous population which came with the state of peace was to some extent satisfied.

1836–40:
Another decline as a result of several years of crop failure.

1841–45:
A marked rise in the number of marriages as a result of particularly favourable business conditions.

1846–50:
Not such a marked rise in the number of marriages on account of dearth and other unfavourable conditions.

27 Now I must present my own opinion. Naturally it is indisputable that the economic situation, wealth and business conditions, crop failures and good seasons etc. will have an influence on the number of

---

[7] My Table 1 also shows that the number of marriages was a great deal lower, especially in 1847, than in the immediately preceding years. Nevertheless, the number was still higher than in any single year before the five years 1841–45, when the great increase began.

marriages in a country. This can be seen quite easily from the totals for individual years. For example (see Table 1) the small number for 1814 and the large one for 1815 (the change-over from war to peace); low totals in 1838 and 1839 as compared with the immediately preceding years (bad and better seasons); a large number for 1846 and a smaller one for 1847 (good times and bad times). What applies to a single year can also apply to a greater period of time. The total for the five years 1836–40 would certainly not have sunk as low as it did, had several bad years not occurred, and the totals for the five years 1841–45 would certainly not have risen so high, if there had not been such a series of good years. But not everything is explained in this way. Indeed not even the essentials. I am of the opinion that the rate of increase in the number of marriages and with it the increase in the population in the course of this half-century, is, to a great extent, independent of the favourable or unfavourable conditions prevailing at a particular time. I believe it likely that if there had been no war, nor any other adverse circumstances in the years 1807–14, there would nevertheless have occurred a considerable increase in the number of marriages in the years between 1815 and 1825. Even if there had been very good times from 1836 to 1840 and hard times from 1841 to 1845, it is probable that the totals would still have been pretty low in the former and quite high in the latter period. Indeed, I can state my opinion, a very happy one at that, in this way. It must be considered one of God's mysterious designs that the war ended in 1814, just when, from 1815 onwards, a much greater number of families was established than before, whose fathers and breadwinners, had they been established earlier, would have been still harder pressed by the hardships of wartime. I believe too, that in the same way, it was very fortunate that the unusually long series of bad years between 1835 and 1840 ended just at the time, from 1841 onwards, when again a much greater number of families was established than before. On the other hand, by way of contrast to these benefits, I must also mention those acts of God which produced the dearth of 1847 and the many perplexities brought about by wars and rumours of war in 1848. For these occurred just at the time when an unusually large number of new families were established, many of which must be feeling anxious and threatened at the present time.

5

The relationship between the past and the present

28 What grounds there are for the opinion I presented at the end of the last chapter, I shall now try to show through the evidence I have collected and my observations upon it.

To begin with we must turn to the particulars which appear below in Table 12. Before, however, directing the reader's attention to the table, I must give some explanation of it. From 1801 onwards, the totals are taken from printed and reliable tables.[1] Before that time the reliability is less as in the last century not so much attention was paid to these matters. The priests' and bishops' lists of births and marriages were not wholly accurate; not all the totals were preserved in printed books and the handwritten lists are now, for the most part, lost. So we lack details of marriages for most years of the last century except for the Christiania Diocese, and even there the totals of the children born are missing for individual years at the end of the century. These gaps I have been forced to make good by guesswork.[2] In spite of this, I still

[1] Several foreign writers have asserted that one does not get reliable statistics on population conditions, so long as the work involved in collecting the material together is entrusted to the clergy. In various countries, therefore, the task has been entrusted to civil officers. But this objection against the reliability of the tables does not apply to our country, where nearly all the inhabitants belong to one and the same church, and where, according to both civil and ecclesiastical law, it is one's duty to report all births, deaths etc. to the priest concerned.

[2] In *Materialien zur Statistik d. danischen Staaten*, 2nd pt, 1784–86, is to be found, for all the dioceses and for the entire kingdom, lists of births and deaths from 1735 to 1784 as well as of marriages and illegitimate births for the years 1770–84. Details of births for the whole kingdom, but not for the dioceses, are continued up to and including 1792 in Schlegel's *Statist. Beskrivelse af de fornemste europ. stater*, 2nd pt, p. 28. For the Christiania Diocese there is a defective series of bishops' and deans' lists of marriages etc. from 1733 onwards.

This is the material I have found. First of all I have produced the table for the Christiania Diocese. The materials are wanting so far as marriages are concerned in the years 1744, 1749, 1750, 1757 and 1760, as well as for both births and marriages for the years 1786, 1787 and 1793. For these years I have used the average of the other years in the same five-year group. Next I have produced the table of births for the entire kingdom. The great gap for the years 1793–1800 I have filled up in this way. The number of births in the Christiania Diocese is a

Table 12. *Five-yearly totals of marriages and of live births in the diocese of Christiania and in the kingdom of Norway, 1736–1850*

Years	Christiania Diocese		Kingdom of Norway	
	Marriages	Live births	Marriages	Live births
1736–40	10,571	44,980		100,456
1741–45	10,419	40,557		95,989
1746–50	11,261	44,667		105,174
1751–55	12,408	49,034		117,233
1756–60	11,210	51,188		120,955
1761–65	12,311	52,823		123,665
1766–70	12,356	52,936		120,854
1771–75	12,063	47,543	25,446	107,997
1776–80	13,778	53,979	31,418	116,627
1781–85	12,829	51,900	30,077	116,182
1786–90	15,046	56,904		121,271
1791–95	15,755	62,295		136,184*
1796–1800	14,386	62,325	34,313*	137,615*
1801–05	14,191	54,418	33,917	125,948
1806–10	13,269	54,405	31,389	123,977
1811–15	17,011	58,274	37,129	124,677
1816–20	18,300	69,333	41,583	154,507
1821–25	19,527	79,531	44,081	170,654
1826–30	17,506	80,928	42,558	179,898
1831–35	17,210	77,438	42,233	181,363
1836–40	16,573	73,106	40,681	171,623
1841–45	21,546	82,759	50,590	195,401
1846–50	22,958	94,058	52,506	210,887

* After this table was prepared and after the present essay, in which the figures from the table are frequently used, was all but written, I unexpectedly came across two papers, which contained the number of marriages and births for the latter part of the last century. From the aforegoing remarks, one will have noticed that I lacked details of births in the kingdom for the years 1793–95, as well as for the years 1796–1800, and that I was myself forced to fill the great gap, questionable as such a procedure is, by a kind of calculation, or to be more correct, by guesswork. I make haste therefore to add an explanation of the extent to which the lately discovered data agrees with my guesswork.

believe that even for the last century the table is good enough to give us a reasonable insight into the essential character of the matter upon which we are engaged here.

very large fraction (almost half) of the total for the entire kingdom. I knew what this fraction was for the years 1776–90 and 1801–15, and assumed from this that it must be the same for the three years 1793–95 and for the five years 1796–1800. The total which was calculated according to this supposition agreed very well with the considerable rise in the number of births that had taken place in the last five years, of which I had details. This number rose evenly in 1787–92 from 23,070 to 28,246. (On this see the footnote to Table 12, which was appended later.) The details referred to on marriages in the kingdom as a whole for the period 1770–84 are used in the table as if they applied to the years 1771–75, 1776–80, 1781–85.

The two particular papers are:
(1) A French one. In Paris in 1802 there appeared a work by a certain Catteau, *Tableau des États Danois* (pt 2, p. 95)
(2) The German translation of a statistical survey of Denmark by the well-known Fr Thaarup *Versuch einer Statistik der dänischen Monarchi*, Copenhagen 1796 (second edition pt 1, p. 4). This translation was produced by the author and was a somewhat extended version of the first edition.

In Thaarup I found a list of births and deaths for the whole of Norway for the years 1785–94. In Catteau I found a list of births and deaths for the years from 1785 to 1799 as well as a list of marriages for the years 1795–99. With a couple of minor exceptions the two writers agree as to the totals. Here I keep to Catteau's list, as it covers the longest series of years.

According to these lists, the number of marriages in the five years 1795–99, which almost corresponds to the five years 1796–1800 in the table, was 34,313. Furthermore, the number of births:

in the five-year period 1786–90 was 121,413
in the five-year period 1791–95 was 137,972
in the five-year period 1795–99 was 138,797

If we now assume that the total in the five years 1795–99 was somewhat similar to the total in 1796–1800, then we can compare the totals for these three five-year periods with the corresponding ones in the table prepared by me, and we will then find that the totals which I adduced by guesswork for 1791–95 and 1796–1800, great as they are by comparison with those that preceded and those that followed them, are not too great, but too small. The fact that the number of births in the last two five-year periods of the last century was very great, is of much interest for the following presentation. It is fortunate too that I have now been able to prove that I had not set the number too high.

In some places in this essay I have by changes in the original manuscript used the later-discovered data of Catteau.

29 If we now cast a glance at the totals, the first thing we notice is the naturally well-known circumstance that, when the number of marriages increases, so does the number of children that are born.[3] Another feature deserves particular notice, namely that when the number of marriages has continued to rise over a somewhat longer period, then the corresponding increase in the number of births begins some years after that and continues some years longer. In the Christiania Diocese, for example, the number of marriages already began to rise in the period 1811–15 and was to continue to do so until 1825, when it reached its peak and began to fall. The number of births, on the other hand, first began to rise in the years 1816–20 and reached its peak in the years 1826–30. We find more or less the same thing happening in the figures for the kingdom as a whole. Here, too, the number of marriages reached its peak in the years 1821–25, but the births not until 1831–35, i.e. about ten years after.

30 And now at last I come to the matter which is my real concern in this chapter and for which I shall make good use of Table 12.

[3] These totals of births undoubtedly include the children born outside marriage. Due, however, to their small number the situation referred to is not affected. More on this in another place.

When, perhaps, for several years in a row good times have prevailed in a town or country district, when flourishing business results in an unusually large number of new families being founded, then one can see half a score months later an unusually large number of children creeping and crawling about the streets and farms. 'The cry of the young is everywhere', one hears people say, and one is surprised when all of a sudden the crowd appears so numerous. 'Surely there were not so many ten years ago?' What now? Some of the many children do indeed die in their early years, for it is with the human race as with a blossoming apple tree, many of the blooms fade and fall to the ground without bearing fruit. But most of the children live and reach adulthood. And, one knows, 25 years after his birth a man is 25 years old. Just as suddenly then as the cry of young children began in every corner, so in due time – it is about 25–30 years later – a great number of young people enter the marriageable age groups and the majority of them marry. The priest is astonished at the number of couples he has married this year and last. The farmer shakes his head at the number of newly married people, finding perhaps that his outfield is already too small to provide pasture for any more animals, never mind marking out new plots so that young people can clear land and make themselves a home. The handicraft master maintains that the many journeymen who now want to marry and set themselves up as Free Masters will make it impossible both for themselves and for the old Licensed Masters to live. On all sides one sees that times are hard and difficult for this increasingly numerous crowd. It can happen that some young people discover this themselves and choose perhaps to go to another country, to America. But the majority will remain in the country and the majority will marry.

This is now a common enough view, but it affects not only a single town or country parish, where some people may have experienced some such thing[4] and arrived unaided at such a view of the matter, it affects the whole country.

31 In the years 1815–25 an unusually large number of people, as is frequently remembered, established families. As one would expect, the number of children born increased very considerably, from 124,000 in the years 1811–15 to 154,000 in the years 1816–20, that is 30,000 more. It was then to be expected that in the years 1841–45 there would be a much greater number of people in the 25-year age group than

---

[4] It was whilst reflecting on the conditions in Lom and Vaage in Gudbrandsdalen, that it first came to me to see the connection between the past and the present (see the end of para. 20).

in the period 1836–40, since these years were just 25 years after the ones in which the many children were born. But when there are many people in the aforementioned age groups, then it is both to be expected and hoped for that many, little by little and mostly in the ages between 25 and 30, will have both the inclination and the means to marry and establish families. It is quite natural that in hard times, when it is more difficult to make a living, some are induced to put it off for a year or two, but in normal times it is to be expected that more marriages will be established when the number of people in the marriageable age group is larger. And Table 12 shows that in the years 1836–40, when, as we have stated, the number of marriageable people was bound to be lower, so too was the number of marriages. But the number of marriages was greater, and much greater at that, in the years 1841–45 (and likewise in 1846–50) when the number of marriageable people was greater. Indeed when we look at Table 1, we see that the number of marriages rose very steeply just from 1841 onwards, in much the same way as the number of births rose very suddenly in the corresponding earlier period.

32 Generally speaking it is not really correct to put the marriages and births into fixed five-year periods as I have done for the five years 1801–05, 1806–10 etc. and then to carry out comparisons such as those above. This comparison can usually be carried out somewhat more exactly and will then show even more plainly why, for example, it was to be expected that in the years 1836–40 far fewer marriages would take place than in the years 1841–45. The fact is that most men do not marry at precisely 25 years of age. One will come closer to being correct if one takes the age mid-way between 25 and 30 years ($27\frac{1}{2}$ years).[5] From now on it will be understood that the men who married in the years 1836–40 must have been born, not in the years 1811–15, but at the earliest in the years 1808–12. But it was in just those years that a much smaller number of children were born (only 121,007) than in any other period of the same length since the beginning of this century. And this is not the only thing to be remembered at this point. In those years, the worst war years, mortality was greater than at any other period for several generations. Furthermore this high mortality occurred especially amongst the small children, the reason for which must probably be sought, not only in the poor nursing which in that pressing time could be rendered them, but also in the fact that in

[5] This age is just about right so far as the bachelors are concerned. As against them, the number of widowers who remarry is quite small. But more on this later.

the suffering which affected everyone in the country, and therefore also those who became mothers, many children were undoubtedly born weak and with little chance of survival. Indeed there is reason to believe that the mortality experience of the cohort of those years, owing to these circumstances, continued to be somewhat greater than usual, even after the distress and hard times were over.[6] However, as unusually few children were born in the years 1808–12 and as an unusually large number of them died at an early age, it is obvious that 28 years later, or in the years 1836–40, there would be an unusually small number of men in the 28-year-old age group, and consequently unusually few marriages. This supposition accords very well with the fact that it was actually in these same years that a lower number of marriages was established than in any other period of equal length since 1815. It must also be assumed that the number of marriages was likely to be somewhat smaller than it otherwise would have been because as noted earlier, the years 1836–40 saw some bad seasons. But from what has been said it seems clear that even if there had been an uninterrupted run of good times, both at that time as well as before and afterwards, the number of marriages must have been lower in 1836–40 than either before or since. Furthermore, with regard to the particularly sharp increase in the number of marriages from 1841 onwards, it ought to be recalled that, just at the corresponding time 25–30 years before, vaccination was no longer a recent introduction but was more generally spread and the result was that multitudes of children were kept alive who otherwise would have been hidden in an early grave.

33 From 1826 to 1840, for three five-year periods in a row, fewer and fewer people were married, the number falling from 42,500 to 40,500 couples. From 1841 onwards the number rose suddenly to 50,500 (1841–45) and 52,500 (1846–50). Furthermore it appears that in the five years 1851–55 it will remain at the same high level. Suddenly therefore, the number of newly established families rises by 10,000 in five years. This is a very remarkable event, no matter whether we look at it from the standpoint of the reasons or the results. For the moment we are dealing with the reasons. Other men have sought these

[6] I have somewhere – I believe in Bernoulli's *Populationistik* – seen the remarkable observation made about one of the German states, that when the draft board came to the cohort whose year of birth is known to have been one of distress throughout the whole of Europe, namely 1816, the proportion of small and sickly men who presented themselves before the board was seen to be much greater than in the other cohorts. If the bad times in which this cohort was born could affect the stature and health of the adult population in this way, then it is likely that its effects brought many of the young people to the grave.

in contemporary happenings, in the favourable or unfavourable circumstances that made it difficult or easy for people to find a livelihood, as for instance the crop failures in several of the years 1836–40 and the good seasons in 1841–45. I have not overlooked the influence of these circumstances, but have pointed out besides that the number of marriageable people, without whom there would not be any marriages, must have been less before and greater after 1841 and that the reason for this is to be sought 25–30 years earlier. This comment applies to the entire kingdom and from the table one can see that it applies also to the Christiania Diocese. It is only because I do not wish to tire the reader with too many totals that I have not shown that the same applies also to all the remaining dioceses, indeed for individual deaneries and parishes.

34 But now one wonders: is it possible that the great increase in the number of marriages that occurred in the ten years immediately following 1815 can also be explained, at least in part, in the same way, namely as a result of a marked increase in the number of children born at a corresponding earlier period? And it is with this question in mind that I have in Table 12 continued the totals of marriages and births back as far as possible into the previous century.

Some of the people who were married between 1815 and 1825 could quite easily be foreigners who moved here after the peace. But one has never heard that there were very many of them. The majority of marriages were fairly certainly those of the country's own children. When we remind ourselves of the fact that they were probably between 25 and 30 years of age when they married, then we discover that the majority of them were born in the last ten years of the previous century. Now the country suffered under a destructive war in the years just before 1815, and immediately afterwards there were comparatively good and prosperous times. But we could, for a moment, look away and imagine that times were good both before and after 1815. We may then say that if in the last ten years of the eighteenth century more children were born than usual, and if no special child sickness occurred that would diminish the total, then it would be expected that in the ten years immediately following 1815, there would be more marriageable persons and, from them, more newly married couples would emerge than usual.

Table 12 shows us that the number of children born in the last ten years of the eighteenth century was markedly greater than in both the period preceding and the one following these years. Certainly the totals for this period are less reliable, as we have said before, in particular so

far as the kingdom as a whole is concerned. Nevertheless if we look at
the totals for the Christiania Diocese, it becomes fairly certain that
what we supposed did in fact occur.[7] We see also the reason for the
considerable increase in the number of children. For there was a sharp
rise in the number of marriages. Now one remembers what the period
was! It was the age of Christian VII. They were the best years that
Norway had enjoyed for a long time. Good seasons without a break
and a prosperous peace, whilst most other countries of Europe found
themselves at war. This brought blessings throughout the land, a prosperity and contentment which even yet is remembered, not only by the
descendants of the coastal population who were enriched by the profitable navigation, but even by the mountain farmer in the innermost
corner of the country. In such a good time as this, the prosperity of the
people is usually marked by the fact that mortality in all age groups,
and therefore also amongst the newly born children, is lower. And this
is seen also in the same lists from which the totals in the table are taken.
In the Christiania Diocese there died yearly an average of:

in the years 1781–85:	9,008
1788, 1789, 1790:	10,082
1791, 1792, 1794, 1795:	8,096
1796–1800:	8,599
1801–05:	9,265
1806–10:	12,583
1811–15:	9,079
1816–20:	8,086
1821–25:	8,201

So far as the Christiania Diocese is concerned (and it comprises half
the kingdom) our conjecture works out rather well. More children
were born in the years 1791–1800 than usual and not so many as usual
died. As, 25–30 years later, there must have been many marriageable
people, one would expect many marriages.[8]

---

[7] A proportion of the still-births, but by no means all, appear to be included
amongst the live births; the lists are not clear on this. In order to be sure, one can
subtract 1,000 from the totals of each five years. Even then the totals will be
much greater than usual.

[8] In the footnote to Table 12, I remarked that I had found the totals of deaths for
the entire kingdom at the end of the last century. I can now show, so far as the
entire kingdom is concerned, just as above for the Christiania Diocese, that mortality in the years 1791–95 and 1796–99 was less than in the years immediately
preceding and following. The average yearly total of deaths was:

in the five years 1786–90:	20,124	1806–10:	23,953
1791–95:	18,545	1811–15:	21,386
1795–99:	18,906	1816–20:	17,894
1801–05:	21,584	1821–25:	18,938

35 What we have said so far can be summed up briefly as follows:

(1) An increase in the number of births 1791–1800 leads to an increase in the number of marriages about 25 years later, i.e. 1816–25.

(2) A reduction in the number of births from 1801 to about 1815 and besides that a high rate of mortality amongst them, leads to a reduction in the number of marriages 25 years afterwards, i.e. from 1825 to 1840.

(3) A marked increase in the number of births from 1815 onwards and a low rate of mortality so that a greater number than usual reached adulthood, leads to a marked increase in the number of marriages about 25 years later, i.e. from 1841 onwards.

36 It is like the swell on the sea. A sea's surface is as calm and shining as a mirror. A gust of wind presses the water down in a particular place and so, by its side, a wave is raised into the air. It reaches its peak and sinks back, but in doing so forces up another wave by its side. A new gust of wind can drive this last wave even higher and the up and down movement can be continued for a long time. How high the swell rises and how long it continues depend upon the wind and the current, the breadth and the depth of the sea – in short upon a multitude of circumstances. To calculate the movement or to discover the laws governing the water's flow is assuredly an object of constant attention for naturalists. But here I continue with the study of the population movements in our country.

Twice in this century has the number of marriages risen both sharply and over an appreciable length of time, namely in the ten years after 1815 and after 1840. I have expressed the opinion that this is something that was to be expected after a similar increase in the number of births at certain, corresponding, earlier periods of time. With that I have accomplished what I particularly wanted to do in this chapter. But when the opportunity offered, I also collected the data covering the movement of population in our country for a still earlier period and have put upon them an interpretation, by which the movements which have occurred in the present century can be explained as the continuation of movements which lie further back in time. I therefore devote another couple of pages to the presentation of this conjecture. If my words give rise to other and more successful enquiries which would carry these investigations further, then they would contribute to shedding considerable light upon the fortunes of past generations in our country.

The interpretation I venture to put forward is based essentially upon

the totals of births in Table 12. These totals appear somewhat differently, however, when they are presented as five-yearly totals for the
years 1735–40, 1741–45 etc. as against the years 1738–42, 1743–48
etc. These different methods of computation are to be found in
Table 13.

Table 13. *Five-yearly totals of live births in Norway, showing
the peaks and troughs, 1735–1850*

Years	Totals		Years
1735–40	100,456	*96,443*	1738–42
1741–45	*95,989*	100,210	1743–47
1746–50	105,174	110,633	1748–52
1751–55	117,233	120,190	1753–57
1756–60	120,955	121,827	1758–62
1761–65	**123,665**	**122,847**	1763–67
1766–70	120,854	115,952	1768–72
1771–75	*107,997*	*108,303*	1773–77
1776–80	116,627	120,157	1778–82
1781–85	116,182	115,134	1783–87
1786–90	121,271	128,837	1788–92
1791–95	137,184	**137,615**	1793–97
1796–1800	**137,615**	131,523	1798–1802
1801–05	125,948	131,361	1803–07
1806–10	*123,977*	*121,007*	1808–12
1811–15	124,677	135,819	1813–17
1816–20	154,507	158,983	1818–22
1821–25	170,654	175,163	1823–27
1826–30	179,898	177,979	1828–32
1831–35	**181,363**	**181,947**	1833–37
1836–40	*171,623*	*177,842*	1838–42
1841–45	195,401	202,111	1843–47
1846–50	210,887	216,867	1848–52

Essentially what we must take note of in this table is that there is a
certain interval between the highest and lowest total that, to stick to
the image we have used before, indicates the highest and lowest points
of the swell. So this can be seen more easily I have printed the higher
totals in bold characters and the lower ones in italic (see Table 13).
What we are now ready to investigate, with the help of these totals, is
whether there is a regular interval between two of the lowest and two
of the highest totals so that we may believe there to be a connection
between the one interval of time and the other, in much the same way
as there is a connection between the rise and fall of the waves in the
sea, a movement directed by an unchanging natural law.

If we begin with the first column, going from top to bottom, and
count the years from the middle of the first to the middle of the second

five years, then we find the first low total is in the years 1741–45, the next is thirty years afterwards in the years 1771–75, the next is 35 years after that in the years 1806–10 and finally another 30 years elapses to the years 1836–40. Four times, therefore, the wave sinks, and with an interval of at least 30 and at most 35 years between each movement.

In the same way one finds that the wave rises three times and that there is an interval of at least 30 and at most 35 years between each peak.

On the whole, we find the same applies to the other column where the totals are arranged for the years 1738–42 etc. The largest deviation is in one instance where there is an interval of 40 years.

We find, therefore, an extraordinary regularity when we compare the points of time at which the highest and lowest totals occur. The totals rise and fall regularly, so that the movement appears like a swell with the one wave, as it falls, pressing up another by its side, so that all go forward in a row. And however one tries to explain the situation, so must one remember that from the multitude of children born at the beginning of the period, which neither death took away nor emigration carried out of the country, came the parents and grandparents of those born at a later period or, conversely, the children born, for example, in the years 1841–50 were for the most part, the children, grandchildren and great-grandchildren of those born in the earlier periods.

37 In this connection, we must consider how long a period of time can be said to elapse between the different generations of parents, children and grandchildren. And if it should be discovered that this period more or less corresponds to that regular interval we have noticed between the highest and lowest totals, then it would not be unreasonable to try to explain the matter simply by saying that, under normal circumstances, the greater the number of parents, the greater the number of children and the greater the number of grandchildren there will be.

It will naturally never be possible to separate the cohorts of the different years with any great accuracy, since they are for the most part too entangled. But we may *a priori* establish what can reasonably be considered to apply.

And it is reasonable to believe that of the children of a particular cohort who reach adulthood and marry, the majority will marry between the ages of 25 and 30 years. Some marry at an earlier age and mix themselves, so to speak, with the children of an older cohort, but this is counterbalanced by the fact that the cohort which in that way gives up something to an older one, also gets a contribution from the older cohort, since some people marry at a later age than usual. We also know that most children are born in the first five to ten years after their parents' marriage.[9] If it happens that for five years in a row many people marry and that in the next five years few people do so, then it is to be expected that a greater number of children will be born of the many marriages in the first five years, than of the fewer marriages in the second five years. And furthermore this will show itself about five years, or perhaps somewhat more, after the marriage. In order to express myself briefly, I can put it this way. If there occurs at a certain period a small number of births in the country, then there will, all things being equal, 25–30 years later occur a small number of new marriages, and 30–35 years later a small number of births.

I set therefore 30–35 years as a reasonable period between the consecutive generations of parents, children and grandchildren.[10] A gap of this magnitude, is, however, very similar to that between the pairs of highest and lowest totals as shown in Table 13.

38 If we believe, therefore, that these assumptions about the usual ages at which people marry and become parents are valid, and if we suppose for a moment that there have been, right from 1735 to the present day, unexceptionable times, so that neither crop failures nor

[9] In Table 12 we see that in the Christiania Diocese the maximum number of marriages occurred in the years 1821–25 and the maximum number of births in the period 1826–30. For the kingdom as a whole, the former occurred in 1821–25, the latter in 1831–35, that is, ten years later.

[10] After this was written I found a publication which, on the whole, agrees very well with the view put forward here as to the usual period between a generation of parents and children, or of children and grandchildren. In Sweden, where the conditions in this matter must be more or less the same as ours, one knows the ages of the women who become mothers. In the years 1836–40, the average yearly total of women who bore children was 95,876, and of these there were:

under 20 years:	1,382.4
between 20 and 25:	14,317.0
between 25 and 30:	24,879.8
between 30 and 35:	24,451.2
between 35 and 40:	19,349.8
between 40 and 45:	9,966.6
between 45 and 50:	1,503.0
over 50:	26.2

If, instead of these age groups, we think of the specific ages: 19, 22.5, 27.5, 32.5, 37.5, 42.5, 47.5 and 51, one can find the average age of all these mothers. It is almost 32 years (31.8). The fact that some women bear children at a younger, others at an older age, cancels out. So far as the majority of the children are concerned, then, one can say that they are born of mothers who are 32 years old or thereabouts. If we think now that in a certain period exceedingly few children are born, there will be few adults (and naturally also few adult women). It is then to be expected that there will be few mothers in the new generation, and this will show itself in particular about 32, or to use round figures, 30 to 35 years after the birth of the cohort. After a small cohort there will, in all probability, follow an equally small one, and that after a period of about 30 to 35 years.

war have checked, nor commercial prosperity and other unusual good fortune have advanced, the growth of population, then we could explain the curious rise and fall in the number of children born, as Table 13 shows, fairly accurately, by applying the rule that many parents must, in aggregate, beget more and that few parents must, in aggregate, beget fewer children and grandchildren. In this way one sees how demographic changes in our country are linked from 1735 to the present day.

There are, in my opinion, two ways of explaining the course of population movements, or the changing rise and fall in the number of marriages and births. On the one hand, it can be explained by external circumstances, on the other, by internal ones. By external circumstances I mean the good and the bad times, good seasons, business prosperity and war etc. By the internal circumstances I mean the different ways in which the population can be built up, so that for instance at a certain period of time there could be a comparatively numerous body of young people in the marriageable age groups, at another time a small one. While the external circumstances have their causes in contemporary events, the internal circumstances have their causes in events which occurred at certain earlier periods.

39 After repeating the proviso that, because of the inadequacy of the information relating to this matter, one cannot speak with any absolute certainty, but only advance hypotheses, I now employ this double image to throw light upon the population movements in our country.

In the years 1741–45, we see in Table 13, the number of births was at its lowest. Naturally there was a reason for this and it probably lay in the events that were known to have occurred just then. These years must have been a time of unusual suffering in Norway. This can be understood by the fact that mortality was unusually high at that time. The annual number of deaths was on average:

in the years 1735–40:   15,962
　　　　　　 1746–50:   17,562

but in most of the years 1741–45, or more correctly from 1740 onwards, the number increased dramatically to:

in the year 1740:   17,853
　　　　　　 1741:   24,378
　　　　　　 1742:   44,254
　　　　　　 1743:   18,616

Mortality on anything like that scale has not prevailed in any years from that day to this. The worst years in this respect were the famine year 1773, about which, even now, here and there, one hears appalling reports (35,362 died); the war year 1809, when dysentery was at its worst (32,486 died); the famine year 1813, after the crop failure of 1812 (26,598 died); the hard year 1839, after some poor seasons (26,652 died); and 1848 after the dearth of the previous year (27,916 died). To fully comprehend how the mortality in 1742 must have been so much greater than in any of these following years, it must be remembered that the population in 1742 was very much lower than later and at the highest estimate could scarcely have been more than 650,000.[11] So that in actual fact a fifteenth part of the population was carried off in that single horrible year. This misery was the result of a series of crop failures that hit the whole of Northern Europe. Furthermore, it can be seen from the burial registers that this excessive mortality occurred in every Norwegian diocese. The least affected was the Bergen Diocese, the reason perhaps being that just at this time, at any rate in Søndmør, the fishing was unusually good, both of cod and of herring, 'so that God apparently opened a larder in the sea, whilst he closed another on land, a blessing that ought never to be forgotten'.[12]

In such a time of terror as there must have been in the years 1741–45, it is likely that the number of children born must have been less than usual, a fact which the table shows. We must also assume that death took away many of this small cohort, so that only a few people from this period grew to adulthood.

40 After these unfortunate years the number of children born grew at an even rate for several five-year periods in a row (see the totals in Table 13). There were perhaps consistently good times for the people then. But after 1761–65 the total falls again, being very much lower in the 1771–75 period. The difference is so great that involuntarily we ask: what can the reason be? Now one thing was that the people, just at this time, were oppressed by their own government to an unusual extent, namely by the so-called Extra Tax, which was ordered in 1762 and lasted until 1772. This was a preposterous tax of not less than eight Danish *shillings* a month for everyone over 12 years of age: not exactly an incentive for poor people to establish families, nor for farmers, for example, to admit new crofters onto their property, seeing that in many cases they must be prepared to furnish the tax for them. Another unfortunate event was the dearth which occurred in 1773, or,

[11] Aschehoug, 'Om Folkemaengden i Norge 1664', *Tidssk. f. Vid. o. Litt.*, 2nd year vol. 5.
[12] Strøm, *Søndmørs Beskrivelse*, printed 1762, 2nd pt, pp. 466 and 475. Strøm reckons the beginning of the bad years from 1740, but speaks of several in a row.

to be more precise, reached its peak in that year. Here then are two contemporary events, which certainly could be expected to have contributed to the decrease in the number of births in the years 1771–75. But there is also that earlier event. For just 30 years before (1741–45) an unusually small number of children entered the world, of which an unusually large number died at an early age: a small cohort from which, therefore, in the years 1771–75 or thereabouts, must be expected a small offspring.

It seems we must follow the totals in Table 13 still further! After the last-mentioned low, the number of births increases and maintains itself at about the same level for three five-year periods. It is known that Norway enjoyed a time of good business during the American War of Independence. It was, however, of short duration and does not seem to have exercised any great influence on the growth of population by an accession of new births. On the other hand, we see that in the five years 1791–95 and likewise in 1796–1800, a considerable increase in the number of births occurred, so considerable in fact, that we must at once seek out the most likely reason. It is to be noted that whilst the total (see para. 28, n. 2) appears to begin to rise as early as 1787 or 1788, it falls immediately at the beginning of the present century in the years 1801–05. What can the reason be, therefore, for that temporary increase?

I have already recalled the golden period during the last part of Christian VII's reign, a time whose unusual prosperity was very likely to be seen in the rapid rise in the population. I now go a little deeper into the matter. The year 1789 produced the French Revolution. This revolution gave rise to war in Europe. More and more states became involved in the war. The Danish–Norwegian state for a long time remained neutral. Norwegian shippers were picking up a highly profitable carrying trade, and those Norwegians producing for export were paid high prices. More ships were set on the stocks and activity in the country districts producing timber for export also increased. The heightened trading activity and prosperity prompted a number of men to follow their inclinations earlier than they would normally have done and so raise families. The number of marriages, therefore, increased and quite naturally the number of children born also increased. But this last-named result of the events of 1789 could not have occurred immediately in that same year. And yet we find that a considerable increase in the number of births actually took place in the year 1789. Moreover that favourable state of business and trade lasted up to the year 1807, when it was suddenly broken off by the fact that our

country finally became involved in the general war. Probably the farmer's hopes were sometimes disappointed when crop failures occurred
in a couple of years at the beginning of the century, but the suffering
caused by this was not so great. For all are unanimous in declaring
that the years 1801–07 witnessed an unusually prosperous era, indeed
even better than at the end of the previous century. As a result, one
would expect that a great number of new births would cause a vigorous
increase in the population at the beginning of this century, an increase
that had begun at the end of the previous one. But, according to the
tables, this was not the case, since we have noted the number of new
births was already down considerably by the five-year period 1801–05.

It will, therefore, scarcely do to explain the remarkably high total
of births shown by Table 13 for the period 1791 (or more correctly
from 1787) to 1800, by merely referring to those prosperous conditions,
to contemporary circumstances, or external conditions, as we have
called them. There seems, on the contrary, grounds for taking into
account the previous circumstances, or internal conditions, which
could be thought to have contributed here. And when we, with this
before our eyes, now cast a glance at the table, then we find the following. In the 30 years, which we supposed to be a generation, or the usual
period between a cohort of parents and children, or of children and
grandchildren, before 1791–95 and 1796–1800 (i.e. in the years 1761–
65 and 1766–70) a numerous cohort came into the world. And 30
years before 1801–05, i.e. in the years 1771–75, only a small cohort
appeared. After the former large cohort one would expect a similarly
large cohort of successors in the years 1791–95 and 1796–1800, and
this we find to be the case. After the latter small cohort a small cohort
of successors was to be expected in the years 1801–05, and in actual
fact this too is what we find.

The cohorts for the years 1806–10 and 1811–15 could by the same
method be shown to have been destined to be small or only moderately
large. The war came and brought about a further – externally determined – reduction. Thus can one explain the connection between the
generations up to the present time, which I have already referred to
above.

I repeat the remark that naturally my calculations are very rough,
since I have only had the totals of births from one five-year period to
the next to work upon. Such calculations and the conclusions we have
drawn from them give rise to the natural desire to use the little
data we have from earlier times to learn what we can about the
fortunes and conditions of past generations. And with this I return

from the obscurities of the previous century to present something in the next section from the circumstances of more recent and clearer times. This I hope will show quite clearly the connection between the generations, a connection which is of so much significance for the present time and the present generation.

6

Stability and change in human life

41 In Table 1 I gave the number of marriages year by year from 1801 to 1850, and I noted that the number was never the same two years running. In fact the difference from one year to the next was at times quite considerable. However, this diversity does not surprise us. We are, on the whole, accustomed to so many changes in life, that we have even come to accept the statement that the only constant factor to be found in human affairs is that there is no constant factor. In the path of the heavenly bodies, in the change of the year's seasons, in the uniform roar of the waterfall, we find a natural constancy and regularity: in human life, in mankind's decisions and actions and fortunes, one does not expect to find such. And this reflection makes it seem to many people a vain task to begin such countings and calculations, as appear in this book, about matters relating to such a variable phenomenon as human life. But everything has two sides, as we shall see.

42 I must here draw the reader's attention to the age at which people marry in this country. Here I speak only about those who marry for the first time, that is about bachelors and spinsters.[1]

Some marry under 20, others between 20 and 25, others between 25 and 30 etc. From 1839 onwards we have data on the age at marriage of everyone. In that year there were 6,691 bachelors who married, mostly with spinsters, others with widows; and of them, 1,848 were between 20 and 25 years old. From this one can calculate that for each 100 of these 6,691, there were 28 in that age group. How many were in that age group in the next year, in the year 1840? There were also 28 for every hundred. In the year 1845 there were likewise 28 and in the year 1846 also 28 for every 100.

---

[1] By this is meant, bachelors who marry spinsters or widows, and by the same token, both the spinsters who marry bachelors and those who marry widowers.

Here then was a considerable regularity and constancy.

'But it could have been a coincidence', one will say.

The number of bachelors who married at the age of 20–30 years was for every 100 marriages:

in the year 1845 ... 43
　　　　　1846 ... 43
　　　　　1847 ... 43
　　　　　1848 ... 43
　　　　　1849 ... 43
　　　　　1850 ... 43
　　　　　1851 ... 43

Surely this was a curious coincidence?

The number of girls who married under 20 years of age was for every 100 marriages:

in the year 1845 ... 5
　　　　　1846 ... 5
　　　　　1847 ... 5
　　　　　1848 ... 5
　　　　　1849 ... 5
　　　　　1850 ... 5
　　　　　1851 ... 5
　　　　　1852 ... 5
　　　　　1853 ... 5

Was this also a coincidence?

In each of the years 1845 and 1846 more couples were married than in any previous year – in all probability for as long as people have lived in Norway. In the second of the two years there was the highest total ever – 11,152. In the next year, 1847, when corn prices were so unusually high, the number of marriages was greater than in any year before 1841, though considerably lower than in the year 1846, namely only 9,890. If we make a separate list of the bachelors married we find that there were:

in the year 1845 ... 9,315
　　　　　1846 ... 9,848
　　　　　1847 ... 8,779

The total in the last year was therefore over 1,000 less than in the previous year. Had not the dearth occurred it is reasonable to assume that the total would not have been so very much lower. We must then suppose that about a thousand bachelors failed to marry in that year because of the conditions prevailing in the country. There was then a great difference between the years in this regard. But now we will see

just how many out of each 100 there were in the different age groups.
We find:

	1845	1846	1847
Under 20 years	1	1	1
20–25	28	28	27
25–30	43	43	43
30–35	18	19	19
35–40	6	6	6
40–45	3	2	2
45–50	1	1	1
Over 50	0	0	1
Total	100	100	100

43 Certainly we must be surprised by this startling similarity. There
is some disparity in individual instances, but this is so inconsiderable
that one could call it an accident. As we shall see later the coincidence
is not quite so great as this, but for the time being we should ignore
the differences and focus our attention on the overriding similarity in
the totals, on the striking evidence we have here of regularity and constancy in human affairs. How are we to understand this? Why is it that
from one year to another there are almost equal numbers of older and
younger persons amongst the otherwise variable number of bridegrooms?

If a king gave orders that each year new troops should be raised, the
actual number depending upon the circumstances of the time, but
according to the rule that in each company of 100 men, there should
be exactly so many young boys and so many fully grown men from
each of the different age groups, then we could understand the regularity of such totals as are given above. Is it in this way that the ranks
of the marriage army are filled? Is it some war commissar who puts in
an appearance at the farms and cottages and mountain cabins and
holds a hearing at a certain time and a certain place where tests, selec-
tions and decisions are made that will determine at what age men shall
marry?

44 Some people are of such a temperament that in them the spirited
element is overriding. Often we see them marrying at an early age.
Others are more, as one might say, rationally minded. They do not
allow themselves to be swayed so much by momentary excitement and
therefore often marry much later. As a result of habit and education
some people are of the opinion that they ought not to establish a family
before they have a reasonable prospect of gaining a considerable income each year. Others make a much smaller claim on life both for

themselves and their families and find that a much smaller yearly income is sufficient. In one circle of society, circumstances and life style are such that a man will spend much more if he takes a wife and sets up his own household than if he lives as a single man. In other circles a man can expect to profit, so far as his daily business is concerned, by taking a wife as an assistant. A very common consideration restraining many men from marrying at an early age is that if they then become fathers they will have neither the means nor the accommodation to provide the education and help for their children that they would wish. Not infrequently, however, one hears the exact opposite, namely, that the people do better if they marry early, for then they have more chance, whilst they are young and able-bodied, of helping their children forward than they would later in life. Several have been such children of luck, as one calls them, that at an early age and without much trouble they have become possessed of that which is necessary to maintain a family. Many others, however, must work for a much longer time in order to reach such a position. Some men, and by no means an inconsiderable number, marry a fortune. But for others it does not happen, or if it does it works against them. Not infrequently it happens that young men are urged either by their parents or others to conclude an advantageous match. It sometimes happens, therefore, that a man has decided to marry and has already made his choice, whereupon family and friends come and try to dissuade or prevent him. One man has the great good luck to secure as his bride just the woman his heart desires, the one above all others he wanted to win. Another may experience a heartache from which he only slowly recovers. Some people develop late, both in mind and body, and are for a long time childlike and immature. Others, on the other hand, develop rapidly so that, at an early age, they possess an unusual degree of independence of spirit, arriving early at the maturity, strength and courage of manhood. Some men bear in their bosom a heart formed for noble love, and understand the great significance of marriages blessed by God, having fully grasped not only the joy and happiness of marriage and domestic life, but also its Holy duties and great responsibilities. Where such a way of thinking is present, a Godfearing caution will lead a man's steps. Others are coarse to a distressing degree. Instinct, not the heart, leads them. Passion, not thought, determines their decisions. In this matter it is said about such people that they live like animals.

45 There are, therefore, thousands of different circumstances, considerations, habits and conditions which bring about the fact that now one person marries at an early age, now another puts it off from year to year. How is it then, as we have seen, that there is such an extraordinary similarity in the proportions marrying in the different age groups from one year to the next? It is to be hoped that only a few people in this country, if any at all, are driven to marry against their will. Much more must we believe that many, yes, by far the greatest number, when they go before the altar to conclude this so-important pact, do so with the happiest, most mature and the freest of wills. What then determines that amongst each 100 bachelors who marry there should be just 43 in the 25–30-year age group, not more, not less; 18, or at most 19, in the 30–35-year age group; 6 in the 35–40-year age group, etc.?

This is indeed a law. There are not many who have thought further about it or made themselves acquainted with all its individual aspects. But it is still a law notwithstanding, and there is no one who is entirely unacquainted with it, not even he who, at a very early age, feels and knows that he is free and has a free will. We speak about the law and acknowledge its existence, when we, half in jest, half in defiance, repeat the proverb: 'Yes, that way shall we all go!' – 'Shall'? Free choice says 'will', but it is the law which says 'shall'.

46 Though we would joke or bid defiance to it, there is forced upon us the suspicion of a deep mystery, of something inconceivable, yet for the deeper consciousness so absolutely real that what we decide and do is at once both the choice of our free and responsible wills and the fulfilment of the common, unalterable and all-powerful law.

The dandelion blooms in the spring. But not every individual stem shoots up from the black earth at the same time. Some stand already with their heads white when others are just opening their multi-petalled flowers – the plant's wedding feast. If we could count all these flowers in the whole of a great valley, then fairly certainly we should find a remarkable situation. When the earth has been free of snow for some days, and the spring sun shines somewhat warmer, then the first golden flower ventures forth and on the same day even more, but still only a few. On the second day the total is greater, and each day come more and more, until the ground is turned yellow by their great numbers. After some time has elapsed only single new flowers push forth, now one then another, until finally the last one brings to an end the cheerful, bright array. And with a greater regularity than most people think, this is repeated year after year, generation after generation. But the connection here is not very difficult to understand. The many thousands of plants are scattered over the hill sides and small valleys and this is more or less the same year after year. From one year to the next

Nature's law applies; that is that the plants which find a place on the dry, sunlit and fertile areas are driven forth more rapidly than those which are in damp spots or in the shade.

With this example we are probably not able to explain that aspect of human life with which we are concerned here but still it is likely to make more intelligible that which the mind, no doubt in vain, endeavours to fathom. For as one's mind suspects and one's faith apprehends, just as certain as it is that the human will advances by its own free choice, so is it certain that at the same time God's will advances, for better or for worse. So the most important thing of all should be that our will be moulded by God's, that what we decide ought to be decided in God.

If we could see through everything then all our senses would be filled with a speechless astonishment, yes, even better, with an adoring admiration at the sight of the great conformity, order and harmony in God's guidance of the world of free people; a harmony which is not less and, if possible, even greater and more impressive than that we admire when we watch the stars' course across the heavens. But our sight is limited and unfortunately it happens all too easily that when we take the individual phenomenon by itself, so as to examine it more closely, then we disturb the beautiful and inspiring image that before was held by our second sight.

47 I shall point out one further thing. There is something else which very often has a wholly unconscious and yet frequently very great influence upon the decision whether or not to marry early. That is the prevalent opinion as to what is permissible and right, what is decent and becoming. These ideas and opinions embrace us tightly on all sides, like the water in which the fish swim, like the air in which the birds fly. But these opinions, which under the hidden hand of God are formed by the interaction of the minds, thoughts, speech and action of a great number of people living together, usually only change very slowly and, for the most part, can be said to be the same from year to year. And, in so far as it depends on this general way of thinking as to whether many or few marry at an early or late age, we are able to understand why the number of people marrying in the different age groups is proportionately the same, time and again. But all the other circumstances and conditions that more or less consciously, but nevertheless constantly, influence people's minds and decisions with regard to getting married are also the things that the All-Powerful and the All-Knowing guides and leads to the advancement of His loving will; just as it is His sun and His rain-filled clouds that permit the host of

flowers, each in its time, to dance with waving colours and a delicate
bell-like ringing across the fields. And yet, just as there is a difference
between plants and flowers in one country and another, there is also a
difference, a steady and constant one, in people's natures and way of
life in different areas. So that, for example, one finds that in our northern country, with its long winter, there seldom or never arises the
thought of marriage at such an early age as in certain southern countries is usual.

48 So we see the connection and understand that, other things being
equal, under the influence of the same habits and the same patterns of
thought, there will be, from one year to the next, a similar number of
young and old amongst those who get married, across the country as a
whole. But suddenly there is a great and radical change of one kind
or another, for example an unusual dearth, where one not only needs
a greater income to buy one's daily bread, but where for many it
becomes more difficult to acquire the means to do so, when nearly all
must save and so have less opportunity of giving the worker his employment and wages. It is then natural, and quite in agreement with
the view we have just expounded, that some of the people who otherwise would have married in that year would now be inclined to delay.
But how does this work out? Is it the younger who put off their marriages, thinking that after all they have age on their side and that
nothing but good can come from being a year or two older? Or is it the
older ones who say to themselves that since they have waited so long
they can wait a little longer, given that times are now so very difficult?
What happens? Is it possible, then, that under such conditions there is
the same proportion of old and young bridegrooms as in the good
years?

The answer to this question we find by looking at the table in paragraph 42, which shows, on the one hand, that in the dearth year of
1847, about 1,000 fewer bachelors married than in the good year 1846
and yet, on the other hand, there was almost the same proportion of
old and young bridegrooms in the year of the death as in the good
year. We must then believe that this circumstance arises as follows. At
the beginning of each year, there are, in each age group, a certain
number of persons who think they will marry in the course of that
particular year. But there are also a certain number, for example 10
per cent in each age group, who have not definitely decided to marry
and whether they do so or not will depend upon how fortunate they
are during the course of the year in their job or business. Now when a
bad year occurs and deprives people of part of their anticipated in-

come, it is that 10 per cent of would-be bridegrooms who are prompted to delay their marriages until better times and this happens in all age groups, both in the older and the younger.

49 We believe then that there is a conformity to law, a constancy and steadiness in human life which brings about such a remarkable regularity in the proportions marrying in the different age groups. This is a fact which ought not to be overlooked when we consider human affairs. But, at the same time, it would be wrong to assume that this conformity to law is the same as saying there is no change, no irregularity whatsoever. Not once, even in inanimate nature, is there to be found perfect immutability. This regularity, order and harmony is the opposite both of blind chance or arbitrariness as it is of a stiff, dead uniformity.

When we, on an earlier occasion, put together the totals of marriages for some years, we were astonished at the similarity between them. If we examine the totals for a longer series of years then we find a constant, regular change taking place.

Table 14. *The percentage of bachelor-bridegrooms aged under 20 years, 20 and under 25 years, 25 and under 30 years in Norway, 1839–53*

Year	Under 20 years	Between 20 and 25 years	Between 25 and 30 years
1839	1.2	28	40
1840	1.1	28	40
1841	1.3	29	40
1842	1.0	29	40
1843	0.9	29	41
1844	1.0	29	42
1845	1.1	28	43
1846	0.9	28	43
1847	0.9	27	43
1848	1.1	26	43
1849	0.7	27	43
1850	0.8	25	43
1851	0.9	25	44
1852	0.7	24	43
1853	0.7	24	43

In Table 14 I set out year for year, from 1839 to 1853, the number of bachelors in every 100 who married, and who were under 20 years of age, between 20 and 25 and between 25 and 30 years. In working out the totals for the first group I used fractions.

Now when we look at the totals in the table, for example, for the first years in the series, 1839 and 1840, we find an almost complete agreement in the totals for the different age groups. The same is also true if we look at the last two years, 1852 and 1853. If on the other hand, we compare the totals for the first and last years, i.e. 1839 and 1853, we do not find such an agreement. But this must not be thought to have destroyed the impression we obtained earlier of a harmony and conformity to law. For, though the totals in the later years are different from those in the earlier ones, the passage between them is an even one, so even in fact that one could not possibly believe that it had come about by chance. The change is as follows. In 1839 somewhat more than 1 out of each 100 bridegrooms (i.e. 1 per cent) were in the youngest age group, that is under the age of 20; but little by little and fairly regularly this percentage of young bridegrooms declined, though of course this could not have been by very much. In 1839 some 28 per cent of the bridegrooms were between the ages of 20 and 25 years, this percentage rose little by little to 29 per cent and finally declined to 24 per cent. The number of bridegrooms between the ages of 25 and 30 years rose from 40 per cent in 1839 to 44 per cent in 1853. Taken on the whole, therefore, the number, or more correctly the percentage of young people, was greatest in the early period, least in the later.

50 After surveying the totals for each single year, and seeing that what change occurred was regular and even, we get an overall view of the situation with the help of Table 15. This sets together in five-yearly intervals the totals for the whole period 1839–53.

Table 15. *The percentage of bachelor-bridegrooms and spinster-brides, in the various age groups in Norway, 1839–43, 1844–48, 1849–53*

Age	Bachelors			Spinsters		
	1839–43	1844–48	1849–53	1839–43	1844–48	1849–53
Under 20	1.1	1.0	0.8	5.7	5.3	5.1
20–25	28.6	27.6	25.1	41.0	40.6	37.7
25–30	40.1	42.9	42.9	31.1	34.0	34.8
30–35	18.8	18.9	21.1	11.8	11.9	14.3
35–40	7.1	5.9	6.6	5.3	4.3	4.7
40–45	2.8	2.3	2.2	2.8	2.1	1.9
45–50	1.0	0.9	0.8	1.5	1.2	1.0
over 50	0.5	0.5	0.5	0.8	0.6	0.5
Total	100.0	100.0	100.0	100.0	100.0	100.0

A little attention to this table shows us certain distinct and regular changes in the totals from one year to another; changes which are almost identical for both sexes. From the first to the second period the totals rise quite strongly in the age group 25 to 30 years but hardly at all in the next group, that is between 30 and 35 years. For the rest, there is a fall in both the older and younger groups. From the second to the third period the rise ceases in the 25–30-year age group and now occurs in the next one, i.e. 30–35 years and appears, though fairly weakly, in the 35–40-year age group. Against this trend, the totals continue to sink in the younger and older groups.

51 When we watch the hour hand move slowly and regularly around the clock face, we know there is a reason for this. The regular change which is in progress in the totals in Tables 14 and 15, the change in the percentages of younger and older brides and bride-grooms, must also be caused by something.

I believe we have a choice of three possibilities:

(1) There is a change in habits and thoughts, causing people to believe that it is not so good to marry at so early an age as before, but that one ought to delay marriage until one becomes a little older.

(2) It could be that in the first part of the period 1839–53 there was a particularly numerous body of young people in the country (i.e. in the 20–25-year age group) and proportionately fewer older people. In the later period the situation was reversed, so that there was a greater number of older marriageable persons and proportionately fewer younger ones.

(3) It is possible that both these occurrences took place; a change both in the manner of thought, and in the composition of the population. The two influences could have worked to the same end, so that from year to year we find a somewhat smaller number of young couples, those under 25 years, and on the other hand a greater percentage of somewhat older ones, those in the 25–30 and 30–35-year age group.

Such could be the reasons for the changes which from year to year show themselves in the totals in Table 15. How was it in reality? This is a question that deserves an answer. But it so happens that the investigations which should serve to resolve this question also help bear out the view put forward in the previous chapter, namely, that the sharp rise, so often spoken about, in the number of marriages from 1841 onwards, is essentially the result of events that happened generations before – the connection between the present and the past, as I have called it. It is for this reason that I have dealt provisionally here with this matter of age at marriage.

7

The course of the population movement

52 'The stream of life' is a metaphor that is often used. It is a good one. It fits the individual whose feelings and emotions follow one another in a continuous stream; sometimes tranquil and calm, like the river in the valley; sometimes wild and roaring like the foaming forest brook. It fits still better an entire people, whose thousands of members are born and live and die, and so move along life's path with that same regularity and momentum as we find when looking at the thousands of drops that make up the mighty advancing flood. Though the metaphor is often used, its meaning is never exhausted. Indeed the more we dwell upon it, the more we think about it in detail, the more new facets, until then unnoticed, offer themselves. Human life is exceedingly diverse and yet is constant in its diversity, just as the laws of the stream are basically the same in the trickling forth of the spring and the whirling of the waterfall. The metaphor may best suit the poet, yet it is not only with him that it finds a home. A paper, the chief object of which is to present reality, must strive step by step to prove the truth of its propositions, but an essay such as the present one, dealing as it does with certain aspects of human life, must at times discuss matters, the intricacies of which can, initially at least, prove difficult to comprehend. In such a situation a metaphor can help render the argument more intelligible. For what is obscure will, so to speak, appear for us in the shape of a familiar natural object, which we can then examine.

53 Think of a river, about 350 miles long, that has its source in a huge, snow-covered mountain. Throughout the winter it will have a fairly small and fairly regular flow of water. But, when spring comes and the snow on the mountain melts, the flow will increase and the water will rise in the river down in the valley. It can happen, that the rise, owing to a sudden change in the weather, such as an unusually warm summery spell, could, in a particular year, occur more quickly and be of a greater magnitude than for many years past. Now if you suppose that along the river there were raised some kind of measuring post, so arranged that one could easily see the height of the water in feet and inches and fractions of an inch, and if you suppose that these poles were placed at certain intervals, for example five miles between each, then it is obvious that the increase in the quantity of water, which would raise the level along the river's entire length, would show itself first at the measuring post that was placed at the highest point in the river, namely at the source. After a certain length of time – if the current ran at one mile per hour, it would be exactly five hours – the rise would show itself at the next measuring post, and so on further down.

54 Now, in the same way, one could pursue the life cycle of some of the families in our country. Birth is the family's beginning. It is possible that, for many years in a row, round about the same number of children are born in one year as in another. But there can occur particular years, indeed even longer periods of time, when a much more numerous cohort comes into the world. This change can occur fairly abruptly. Usually 20, 25, 30, 35 years after a small birth cohort, a small number of people will be found entering the ages of 20, 25 years etc. If, on the other hand, a numerous cohort is born, then one expects, in the fullness of time, that there will be a corresponding increase in the number of 20- and 25-year olds and just as suddenly as the increase in the number of children born showed itself, so will the increase in the number of adults. Naturally this will come about first in the 20-year age group, then five years later in the 25-year age group and so on. No doubt irregularity will occur in one respect. Of the children born not a small number will be carried off by death before they become adults and this number can be greater or smaller in the various cohorts, given that mortality over the course of a number of years can also be greater or smaller. It could also be the case that some of those born in one country emigrate to another and vice-versa. Both these circumstances then will cause some disturbance and the result will be, for example, that people aged 25 years who are to be found in the country at a particular time will not match exactly the cohort born 25 years earlier. But it is not unlikely that this irregularity is no greater, or not much greater, than that which one finds in the course of a river, for this too is subject to variation. For instance some of the masses of thawed snow evaporate or sink into the ground, sometimes more, sometimes less; and besides it is always the case that the river bed, whose shape also has an influence upon the height of the water, will here be wider, there narrower. And yet, notwithstanding all this, we see that under more or less normal conditions, the water level corresponds, as the measuring posts in the river indicate, to the increased or diminished flow from the mountain.

55 But, pursuing this line of thought further, we see that when at a certain earlier period it happens that a small cohort is born, and when, as a result, in the corresponding period that follows there are only a few people in, say, the 25–30 age group, the age at which people for the most part marry, then it is to be expected that generally speaking there will only be a few bridal couples in this same group. And if, on the other hand, at an early period a more numerous cohort came into the world, resulting in an increase in consecutive periods of time of the total of adults in the 20–25, 25–30, 30–35 age groups, then it is to be expected that there will appear a greater number of bridal couples in the 20–25-year age group and later in the 25–30 age group and so on.

When the snow masses melt on the mountain we predict that the water level in the river will rise, and we are able to assure ourselves on this point by measuring the height of the water in feet and inches and fractions of an inch. When, at an earlier time, an increase takes place in the number of children born, then we conclude that an increase will occur in the number of people in the marriageable age groups (20–25), 25–30, 30–35, etc.) and finally an increase in the number of people who actually marry at these same ages. Here too we are able to ascertain the correctness of the theory by measurement. The exercise is carried out by taking the total of married couples who are in the different age groups on their wedding day. From the year 1839 onwards this calculation was in fact carried out by the priests who married them.

56 This work has, in itself, been remarkable enough. For it covered, in the fifteen years 1839–53, no less than 153,561 married couples; or twice that number of individuals, namely 307,122. These were divided into 64 categories.[1] The thought of the difficulty of the work that has already been accomplished – the counting for each single year in each parish and the totalling for the country as a whole and for the entire series of years – will help us overcome the trivial inconvenience that results when we begin to make use of the information that has been won.

---

[1] First of all the many couples are divided in the following four ways:
    (1) Bachelors married to spinsters.
    (2) Bachelors married to widows.
    (3) Widowers married to spinsters.
    (4) Widowers married to widows.
Each of these are further divided into 8 age groups and that separately for each of the two sexes. For the years 1839–45 the totals are given in the census tables for 1845; for the years 1846–53 I have drawn them from the handwritten bishops' lists.

From all the information that has been gathered I give here only those details concerning bachelors and spinsters. The totals of these were:

Year	Bachelors	Spinsters
1839–43	39,519	41,045
1844–48	45,844	48,085
1849–53	47,236	49,245

Naturally, many of these people were not the same age as each other on the day they married. It is important that we should know what their ages were, and how these were apportioned amongst the different age groups.

In order to cast some light on the matter, I give by way of example the number of spinsters in the different age groups:[2]

Age	1839–43	1844–48	1849–53
Completed the 15th but not the 20th year	2,341	2,541	2,483
20–25	16,819	19,506	18,584
25–30	12,779	16,335	17,126
30–35	4,850	5,738	7,057
35–40	2,172	2,066	2,316
40–45	1,143	1,030	954
45–50	618	567	482
50–55	323	302	243
All ages	41,045	48,085	49,245

57 Now we shall take as an example those belonging to the third of the age groups, namely those who have reached their 25th but not their 30th year. In 1839–43, their total was 12,779. Here we ask: when was the bride born who was married on 1 January 1839, and on that date had just attained her 30th year? Answer: 1 January 1809. Further: when was the bride born who was married on 31 December 1843 and had then just reached her 25th year? Answer: 31 December 1818. From this it appears that the brides aged 25–30 years who were married between 1 January 1839 and 31 December 1843, must be assumed to belong to the cohort of female children born during the ten years 1809–18. And from the yearly lists of births, it is possible to get the size of this cohort. It was 127,367.

In the same way, I can discover that the brides in the 25–30-year

[2] In the lists the youngest and oldest age groups are given thus: 'under 20 years' and 'over 50 years'. I have used the more precise limits: 15–20 and 50–55 years. One can be certain that none of the spinsters were under 15 years of age (though it is quite possible that several were as young as 16 years). It can also be assumed that only very few were past their 55th year.

age group, who were married in the next five years, 1844–48, belonged to the cohort born in the years 1814–23; in which years 149,244 female children were born.

The example that I have cited concerning the spinsters who married between the ages of 25 and 30 years, I now give in full in the following short table:

Number of female children born:

1809–18	127,367
1814–23	149,244
1819–28	166,073

Of these the number married in the 25-30-year age group:

1839–43	12,779
1844–48	16,335
1849–53	17,126

If the flow of water in the river is greater in May than in April, owing to the thawing of snow in the mountains, and even greater in June than in May, then one will learn, from the markers placed along the river's length, that the water level rises first in one month and still more so in the next. The same applies to our populations. We see three cohorts of female children: the second greater than the first and the third even greater than the second. After a certain period of time these three cohorts appear as brides in the 25–30-year age group. And the number of brides is greater in the second period than in the first and still greater in the third than in the second. Indeed, if we look still more closely, we see that just as the increase in the children born was particularly marked between the first cohort and the second, so too was the increase in the total married.

58 By this example, therefore, is the procedure explained and we are quickly able to present the comparison between the cohorts of children that were born and the total of marriages that took place later in each of the different age groups. It will be best however, if I first present the number in each of the cohorts that we shall deal with here:

Years	Number of boys born	Number of girls born
1784–93	128,355	122,243
1789–98	138,386	131,794
1794–1803	137,544	131,350
1799–1808	134,086	128,134
1804–13	127,922	122,166
1809–18	133,226	127,367
1814–23	156,408	149,244
1819–28	173,738	166,073
1824–33	181,696	172,789
1829–38	184,728	174,416

After all these preparations I put together all the relevant totals and so demonstrate the truth of the proposition put forward provisionally in the form of the metaphor of a river, which, I said, rises as the flow of water in the higher region increases (see Table 16).

59 Table 16 deserves to be examined with some care. First, let us again find the example presented earlier, the example of the girls who were married in the 25–30-year age group. In the lowest portion of the table, in the column for the 25–30-year age group, the total of those girls is given for the years 1839–43. It was a low total. Then a much greater one appeared in 1844–48 and finally, in the years 1849–53, an even larger one still. And above in the uppermost part of the table we find the corresponding cohorts of newly born girls. The first is the smallest, the second considerably greater, and the third even greater than the second.

Naturally, of these cohorts many died in childhood, and of those who became adults, those we know about, some married when they were in the 15–20-year age group, others in the 20–25-year age group. The rest went on, unmarried, into the 25–30-year age group and of these the number married is the one given above. Even so, there was a residue, still unmarried, which joined the 30–35-year age group and so on.

The same applies also to the bachelors who were married in the 25–30-year age group. In 1839–43 there were 15,859; in 1844–48, on the other hand, there were considerably more – 19,646; finally in 1849–53 even more – 20,282. Accordingly when we look at the totals of male children born (see the top half of the table) we find that the first-named and smallest total of married persons came from the smallest cohort, the second and larger total from the next largest cohort and the third and greatest total from the most numerous cohort of all.

60 In order to facilitate the examination of the table, I have put plus and minus signs to indicate when the totals of births and marriages are greater or less than the preceding period. If we look now at the totals for the persons married in the 35–40-year age group, we see immediately that at first they decrease and then they increase and that this applies both to the men and the women. Accordingly for the cohorts of new-born children we also find first of all a decrease and then an increase.

In the series for the 40–45-year age group, we find the decrease carried on from 1839–43 to 1849–53 and likewise we see that there has been a decrease in the corresponding cohort of children, from the years 1794–1803 to 1804–13.

Table 16. Cohorts of births (1784–1838) and marriages (1839–53) in Norway

These cohorts reached the specified ages (15–20 years etc.) in the years 1839–43; 1844–48; and 1849–53

	15–20 years	20–25 years	25–30 years	30–35 years	35–40 years	40–45 years	45–50 years	50–55 years
Years of birth	1819–28	1814–23	1809–18	1804–13	1799–1808	1794–1803	1789–98	1784–93
	1824–33	1819–28	1814–23	1809–18	1804–13	1799–1808	1794–1803	1789–98
	1829–38	1824–33	1819–28	1814–23	1809–18	1804–13	1799–1808	1794–1803
Births (male)	173,738	156,408	133,226	127,922	134,086	137,544	138,386	128,355
	+181,696	+173,738	+156,408	+133,226	−127,922	−134,086	−137,544	+138,386
	+184,728	+181,696	+173,738	+156,408	+133,226	−127,922	−134,086	−137,544
Births (female)	166,073	149,244	127,367	122,166	128,134	131,350	131,794	122,243
	+172,789	+166,073	+149,244	+127,367	−122,166	−128,134	−131,350	+131,794
	+174,416	+172,789	+166,073	+149,244	+127,367	−122,166	−128,134	−131,350
Age at marriage	15–20 years	20–25 years	25–30 years	30–35 years	35–40 years	40–45 years	45–50 years	50–55 years
Number of marriages: 1. Bachelors								
1839–43	430	11,284	15,859	7,445	2,810	1,102	403	186
1844–48	+448	+12,665	+19,646	+8,668	−2,699	−1,078	*+419	+221
1849–53	*−360	*−11,847	+20,282	+9,973	+3,130	−1,038	−382	*+224
Number of marriages: 2. Spinsters								
1839–43	2,341	16,819	12,779	4,850	2,172	1,143	618	323
1844–48	+2,541	+19,506	+16,335	+5,738	−2,066	−1,030	−567	*−302
1849–53	*−2,483	*−18,584	+17,126	+7,057	+2,316	−954	−482	−243

The years in which the marriages took place

What all this amounts to is that when the birth cohorts increase or decrease then usually the number of those children who in their time marry, decreases or increases in the same way.

61 But no rule is without exception and neither is this one. I have marked with an asterisk in the table those instances where we do not find the expected correlation. There are four instances in the two youngest age groups (two for each sex) and three instances in the two oldest age groups: in all, then, seven instances out of 32. The last three instances could with good reason be excluded from the reckoning, simply because they happen to be in the oldest age groups. Of the children who were born at the end of the previous century and the beginning of this one, there are naturally few who are still unmarried in the years 1839–53, and it is dependent upon all manner of accidents as to how many of these few will finally marry or not. Not much regularity was to be expected here. Statistical calculations can cope with hundreds and thousands, but not very easily with ones and twos. The important exceptions are formed then by the four first-named instances. Among the bachelors and among the spinsters, the number of marriages fell in the years 1849–53 in both the two youngest age groups, that of 15–20 and 20–25 years. This is contrary to expectations since the corresponding birth cohorts had increased, if not by very much.

In the next chapter, I shall come back to these explanations. Here I give only a provisional explanation. In recent times certain unusual circumstances have occurred which have affected the situation and way of thought of young people, the result being that they have become less quick to marry than was the case before (see para. 51, sections (1) and (3)).

62 But with due regard to these exceptions, I put forward the rule that comes out of Table 16, as follows. The number of marriages in the different age groups will, under normal circumstances and in all essentials, be in proportion to the births in the corresponding earlier periods. It is, to recall to mind the metaphor we have used before, just like the water level in the river which will rise and fall in proportion to the amount of snow that some time earlier has thawed on the mountains.

In Chapter 5, I put forward the view that the remarkably large increase in newly established marriages taking place from 1841 onwards was essentially to be explained by the considerable increase in the number of births 25 to 30 years earlier. And at the close of Chapter 6, where I called attention to certain changes in the relationship between the marriages in the different age groups (see Table 15), I indicated that a more detailed examination would establish that view. I now venture to believe that the reader who has had the patience to follow me and who has got a correct grasp of the somewhat complicated detail, will admit that this view seems probable.

63 I cannot, however, support my view by those of other investigators. As I pointed out in Chapter 4, that view is at variance with the explanations given by well-known writers in our own country. Furthermore, in spite of much research, I have not found in the works of foreign writers who have dealt with similar matters any sign of such an opinion as the one I have dared to suggest. Probably one of the most learned essays on the frequency of marriage in any country is a section in some English statistical tables of 1848 concerned solely with marriages in England in the century 1746 to 1845.[3] During this long series of years, the number of marriages had naturally sometimes increased and sometimes decreased and this is explained as a result of the continual changes of war and peace, good and bad business conditions and other sources of livelihood, of activities in the colonies and conquests in other parts of the world, of changes in laws and ministries; in short, of the different circumstances which in any way could be supposed to have any influence upon the welfare of the people and of their prospects. The presentation of all this is so much more interesting because it concerns a nation that has connections with almost all countries in the world and which is therefore influenced by events and changes in even the furthermost part of the globe. As a result, this single essay is not only a contribution to the history of England, but also to the history of mankind in the same period. However, not even in this essay have I found the opinion expressed that an unusual rise or fall in the number of marriages at one period of time is to be explained as a result of an unusual rise or fall in the number of births in an earlier period; nor, that the marked changes in the number of marriages, as I have said before, could be dependent upon both past and present events.[4]

[3] *Eighth Annual Report of the Registrar-General*, London, 1848.
[4] In the English work it is said, for example, that: 'The number of marriages can possibly rise and fall independently of external reasons; but from the foregoing we must conclude that the lists of marriages in England indicate those periods in which times were good as precisely as the stock-exchange dealings measure the hopes and fears on the part of the men of finance. If the stock-exchange dealings are the barometer of credit, so are these marriage lists the barometer of current well-being, and to an even greater extent that which is expected and is being enjoyed beforehand. Therefore the marked rise and fall in the number of marriages in England is the result of peace after war, rich harvests after dearth, high wages after unemployment, active business after flatness in trade, hope after despair, national triumphs after national catastrophes.'

Therefore, I must expect that the wary reader will still have some doubts about what I have put forward. But, on that account, I again dare to hope that the same reader will follow me patiently yet a little further and pay attention to some explanations which should strengthen what in the end will, I very definitely believe, prove to be correct.

64 I shall answer one objection that I think has been made concerning Table 16. My way of thinking was that if the number of new-born children increases suddenly and markedly, then, under normal circumstances, there will, in time, occur a similar increase in the number of adults and in the number that get married. There are three links here: birth – adulthood – marriage. My table groups together only the first and last of these links, i.e. birth and marriage. And to this the objection can be made that it is very risky to conclude that because at one time in the past many children were born so later there should be such and such a number of adults in the country. For it could be supposed that mortality, owing to the prevalence of sickness amongst the children, was very great amongst the numerous cohorts of children, or that many of the children accompanied their parents who had perhaps emigrated to America. In such a situation, a more numerous cohort of children would not necessarily give the country a greater number of adults than would a smaller one. If then many marriages took place in that same generation, then the reason for this must lie, not in the size of the cohort, but in other circumstances; in good years and suchlike, that made it easier for people to establish families.

This objection is quite valid and shows that Table 16 does not contain a wholly conclusive proof of the opinion that I have put forward. I shall, therefore, follow the advice not to jump over the middle link, namely the adults. It must be admitted, however, that the parallel cannot be drawn so finely as before. For I will not be able to divide the people into five-year age groups (e.g. 20–25 years etc.) but must stick to larger groups of ten years.

65 Censuses were held in this country at the beginning of the year 1801, in the spring of 1815 and at the end of the years 1825, 1835 and 1845 (see Table 11). In the first, and the last three of these censuses, children under ten years of age were listed separately, as were young people between 10 and 20 years, adults between 20 and 30 years and so on. For these years, therefore, I know the number of persons, both male and female in, for example, the 20–30-year age group[5] and with

---

[5] For the year 1801 the totals are found in Schweigaard's *Statistik*; for the years 1825, 1835 and 1845 they are to be found collected together in my essay, *Om Dødeligheden i Norge* (*On Mortality in Norway*) app. 1, Table 1.

the aid of data from these last censuses, I can also, with tolerable exact-
ness, calculate how many there must have been in that age group in
1815, when the census was not done in this way.[6]

Here I stick to the totals of persons in the 20–30-year age group. For
both in this and the previous chapter, we have seen that by far the
greatest number of those who marry are in this age group, so that the
small number of newly married couples who are older or younger can
just about be excluded from the calculation. Now, then, I can, in the
same way as in Table 16, group together the totals of (i) new-born
children, (ii) adults in the 20–30 age group and (iii) married people
(Table 17).[7]

66 A fleeting glance at this table shows us the following. Of the five
cohorts of births, and this applies to both males and females, the second
is considerably greater than the first, the third a little greater than the
second, the fourth less than the third and the fifth very much greater
than the fourth. In the same way we find that the number of adults
increased considerably from 1801 to 1815, and from that date until
1825. It declined until 1835 and finally increased very sharply to 1845.
And likewise the number of married people increased greatly in the

[6] In order to show the method I have used, I give some data for males from the
last three censuses. Of these there were:

Year	Aged 20–30 years	Aged 30–40 years
1825	83,704	71,077
1835	82,809	75,761
1845	116,295	76,157

One will understand that those who in 1835 and 1845 were 30–40 years old,
must have been mainly the survivors of those who ten years before, or in 1825
and 1835, were 20–30 years old. (It is assumed that immigration and emigration
made no difference either way.) In the same way the 71,077 men who in 1825
were 30–40 years old must have been the survivors of those who in 1815 were
between 20 and 30 years. This total should be 77,905, if the relationship between 1815 and 1825 was the same as between 1825 and 1835 on the one hand
and 1835 and 1845 on the other. After further investigation, which would be too
tedious to explain here, I have found it more correct to deduct a further 2 per
cent, and so instead of 77,905 put 76,347. It is reasonable to suppose that this
total comes very near the true one, and in any case is hardly likely to be too
great. In the same way is found the number of women who were in the 20–30-
year age group in 1815.

[7] The census taken at the beginning of 1801 I regard as correct for the last day
of 1800, and likewise each of the following censuses as correct for the last days
of 1815, 1825, 1835 and 1845. They, who on those days were 20–30 years old,
are believed then to have been born that number of years before, i.e. in 1771–80,
1786–95 etc. For the last century I have used the recently discovered totals
referred to in the footnote to Table 12. Also, so far as the same periods are
concerned, I have assumed that 105 boys were born for every 100 girls. The
number of adults is set against the number of marriages immediately before and
after each census, i.e. the marriages of the period 1796–1805 and the census of
1801, etc. (See Table 12.)

Table 17. *Cohorts of births (1771–1825), adults aged 20–29 years (1801–45) and marriages (1796–1850) in Norway*

	Years	Male	Female
Number of births	1771–80	115,051	109,573
	1786–95	132,856	126,529
	1796–1805	135,391	129,354
	1806–15	127,060	121,594
	1816–25	166,304	158,857
Adults in the 20–30 year age group	1801	63,934	73,025
	1815	76,347	83,743
	1825	83,704	91,778
	1835	82,809	89,539
	1845	116,295	122,971
Marriages	1796–1805	68,230	
(i.e. an equal number of both sexes)	1811–20	78,712	
	1821–30	86,639	
	1831–40	82,914	
	1841–50	103,096	

second of the five periods – in 1811–20 or around 1815 – increased still around 1825, sank, on the other hand, around 1835 and then increased very considerably indeed around 1845.

It is difficult for one to fail to appreciate that here we are dealing with a law, namely that when the number of births increases or decreases, then in due time the number of adults in the marriageable age groups between 20–30 years increases or decreases, and with them also increases or decreases the number of marriages.[8]

[8] When, for a long period, there have been hard times in a country (war, hunger, pestilence) then necessarily the population is almost stationary. So when good times return, population growth again takes place that much more quickly, with an increased number of marriages and births just as if it was making up for past neglect and filling up the holes. This is an old idea and has been applied to our own country.

In the period 1801–15 we had war, bad harvests, infectious diseases, and the population stood, so to speak, still. In the period 1815–25 there were better times and the population increased rapidly (see Table 11). The stagnation of the population in the former time and its increase in the latter, has been explained as the natural result of the contemporary happenings and of them alone (see Ch. 4). But now Table 17 shows that even in the hard times the number of marriageable persons in the 20–30-year age group increased, so that there were many more of them in 1815 than in 1801. The reason for this lies in the fact that there was a considerable increase in the number of births in the corresponding earlier period, and as a result of this there would, under normal circumstances, have been a greater number of marriages (and therefore of births) around 1815 than around 1801. The marked, indeed the unusually marked, increase in the Norwegian population immediately after 1815, is not, therefore, just the result of the then prevailing conditions (the changeover from war to peace etc.), but also of the events of earlier times which gave rise to the marked increase in the number of births in the years 1786–95 (Ch. 5).

67 Is there still any doubt remaining? Is there still any belief that this accord could possibly be but a remarkable coincidence, or the result of some other, as yet undiscovered, reasons? If so then surely any remaining doubts must disappear if it can be shown that this same accord occurs in different parts of the kingdom – the five dioceses – where any other explanations, for example changing business conditions etc., would be different in the different places. For this reason I have collected together the relevant details. They do not go so far back in time as the ones in Table 17 and for the sake of brevity I have put together the totals for males and females (Table 18).

Table 18. *Cohorts of births (1796–1825), adults aged 20–29 years (1825–45) and marriages (1821–50) in the dioceses of Norway*

	Year	Christi-ania	Christi-ansand	Bergen	Thrond-hjem	Tromsø
Births (girls and boys	1796–1805	116,743	? *	?	?	?
together)	1806–15	112,679	42,918	41,901	32,957	18,199
	1816–25	148,864	52,290	53,747	44,254	26,006
Adults in the 20–30 year	1825	73,939	27,728	30,312	28,030	15,473
age group (men and women	1835	71,444	30,093	30,713	26,025	14,073
together)	1845	105,241	37,631	39,703	35,519	21,172
Married couples	1821–30	37,033	13,376	14,936	13,751	7,543
	1831–40	33,783	13,962	14,894	12,865	7,410
	1841–50	44,504	16,466	17,676	14,977	9,473

* In order to fill in the gaps for the four last dioceses I need details of births for the years 1796–1800. It is possible these could be found in the bishops' archives or in Christiansand's, Bergen's, and Throndhjem's old *Adresse-Aviser*. Communications to me on this subject would be very welcome. [*According to my calculations the missing totals of births are, for the Christiansand Diocese 42,420, for Bergen 44,081 and for the Throndhjem and Tromsø Dioceses combined 60,839. See Michael Drake,* Population and Society in Norway 1735–1865, *Cambridge University Press, Cambridge, 1969, p. 171 – Ed.*]

68 This table, which can be compared with Tables 4, 5 and 6, merits a close examination, for it furnishes quite striking evidence as to the correctness of the rule that the rise and fall in the number of children born leads to a corresponding rise and fall in the number of adults and of marriages. That same rule, which in Table 17 is seen to apply to the kingdom as a whole, applies also to each single diocese. Indeed, we are even able to find an agreement as to the degree of that rise and fall. If the increase of the new-born children is very great, then so is the number of adults and marriages. If, on the other hand, the increase in the number of births is small, then the increase in the number of adults and marriages is also small. This is seen best when we reckon up by how many per cent the number has increased or decreased from one time to another:

		Christi- ania Diocese	Christi- ansand Diocese	Bergen Diocese	Thrond- hjem Diocese	Tromsø Diocese
	Births					
line (1)*	From 1796–1805 to 1806–15	−4	?	?	?	?
line (2)	From 1806–15 to 1816–25	+32	+22	+29	+34	+43
	Adults in the 20–30-year age group					
line (1)	From 1825 to 1835	−3	+9	+1	−7	−9
line (2)	From 1835 to 1845	+47	+25	+23	+36	+50
	Marriages					
line (1)	From 1821–30 to 1831–40	−9	+4	0	−6	−2
line (2)	From 1831–40 to 1841–50	+32	+18	+19	+16	+28

*[*The missing percentages are* +1 *for the Christiansand Diocese;* −5 *for Bergen and* −16 *for the Throndhjem and Tromsø Dioceses combined. See Drake op. cit., p. 171* – Ed.]

Look at the percentage totals for marriages in line 1. They show a small rise for the Christiansand Diocese (+4 per cent), no movement either way for the Bergen Diocese (0 per cent) and some decline for the three remaining dioceses (−9 per cent, −6 per cent and −2 per cent). Look at the totals for adults on line 1 and you will then discover almost exactly the same situation: some increase in Christiansand, almost no increase in Bergen and some reduction in the three remaining dioceses. And a similar reduction occurs also in the Christiania Diocese in the number of births (see line 1).

Look now at the percentage totals in line 2. In all the dioceses there is a considerable increase in the number of married couples, in particular in the Christiania and Tromsø Dioceses. In all the dioceses too there is a considerable increase in the number of adults, i.e. marriageable persons. Again this is especially so in the case of these same Christiania and Tromsø Dioceses. Finally, in all the dioceses in the corresponding earlier period there is a considerable increase in the number of births, in particular in the two named dioceses as well as in the Throndhjem Diocese. In this latter diocese, as we have said, the number of births increased greatly and one would have expected a greater increase in the number of married couples than was in fact the case, bearing in mind the situation in the other dioceses. The increase is indeed marked (+16 per cent), but not to the degree that one had been led to expect. It is therefore reasonable to suppose that some particular circumstances prevented many from marrying in this diocese, so bringing about this break in the normal course of things.

69 These series of figures contain the answer to the vital question which, without them, would remain an enigma. I said 'vital question', for according to the prevailing opinion it is just that rising or falling number of marriages in the country that is the surest pointer to whether a people have or have not a high standard of living and enjoy good prospects, just as the stock exchange index is the best indicator of business prosperity. In Chapter 3, I showed, by means of Tables 4, 5 and 6, how, to a great extent, there is a remarkable parallel between the rise and fall of marriages in the five dioceses. But I also showed that, whilst the number fell slightly in the Christiania, Throndhjem and Tromsø Dioceses in the years 1831–40, it rose somewhat in the Christiansand Diocese and remained about the same in Bergen. Now we must ask: is this to be regarded as proof that the Christiansand and Bergen Dioceses enjoyed better times in those years than the remaining parts of the kingdom, or that the latter experienced one or other forms of distress peculiar to themselves? The answer to this must be no. It appears that, in the course of the years 1831–40, there was in the Christiansand Diocese a more numerous, and in the Bergen Diocese an equally numerous, body of young people as in the years 1821–30, whilst the situation in the other dioceses was the reverse. The reason for this difference must essentially be sought in earlier times, where the same dichotomy had occurred with regard to the number of births.

Why did the number of marriages in the Christiania and Tromsø Dioceses rise so much more in the years 1841–50 than they did in the Christiansand and Bergen Dioceses? Was it solely because trade was flourishing in the former and not so in the latter? I do not know if there was such a difference, but regardless of this it is reasonable to suppose that the number of marriages would be greater in the afore-named dioceses, on the grounds that the number in the marriageable age groups, according to Table 18, had grown the most there.

70 So we come to the most important question: why was there so small an increase or even a decrease in the number of new marriages in the years 1831–40, in the kingdom as a whole and in each of the five dioceses, whilst there was such an extraordinarily marked increase in the years 1841–50? Does this not suggest that times must have been depressing in the former years and flourishing in the latter? If this were so, then one must also say that a great part of the kingdom's youth, the marriageable part in the 20–30-year age group, must have emigrated from the country in the former years whilst a numerous body of young people, in the same ages, must have come here from other countries in the latter. For the census in 1835 found only a few people in that age group; the census of 1845, on the other hand, found many more. But such a migration to and fro has not taken place and so the answer to the question becomes this: in the years around 1835 there were not so many people in the marriageable age group between 20 and 30 years and therefore there could not have been so many marriages, even if times had been of the best. On the other hand, there was a particularly numerous body of young people aged between 10 and 20 years. For each year that passed they became a year older, so that, around the year 1845, they were between 20 and 30 years of age. They had then reached the age at which to marry, and even if times had been hard and prospects gloomy many no doubt would have married. Indeed, instead of being surprised at the large number of people who married in the years 1841–45 in the Throndhjem Diocese – an increase on the previous ten years of not less than 16 per cent – and instead of explaining this as evidence of particularly favourable circumstances in the diocese, one must now turn the question round and ask: what were the unfavourable circumstances that resulted in the increases being so small, as against the other dioceses, when the number of marriageable youth had increased so very considerably (by as much as 36 per cent)?

71 It is – to repeat myself once again – by no means my view that the favourable or unfavourable circumstances of the time have no influence upon people's decision to marry. Only one must not use this alone to explain the greater or lesser number of marriages that occur in any particular period. The totals that have been given probably now show with sufficient clarity that the number of marriages also depends upon the number of people in the marriageable age groups, which number again is for the most part dependent upon the greater or lesser size of the cohort that was born at an earlier time. This view is confirmed again and again, first if one considers the changing number of married persons in the 15–20, 20–25, 25–30-year age groups etc. in the years 1839–53 (Table 16), then if one considers the correlation between the number of marriages as a whole and the population in the 20–30-year age group in the entire kingdom from 1801–45 (Table 17) and finally if one looks at the situation in the individual dioceses from 1825 till 1845 (Table 18).

When the winter snow melts on our mountains in the spring, then the brooks suddenly fill and the small streams grow and steadily but strongly the water level rises in the main stream itself. So it is with the flow of human life. Suddenly, in some earlier period, an increase occurs in the cohort of new-born children. After the requisite amount of time has elapsed the crowd of young, marriageable people also increases and likewise the number of marriages. We find it in the entire kingdom; we find it also, if not quite so regularly and so evenly, in the different parts of the kingdom, whose smaller numbers, taken together, make up the whole.

8

Many — but not relatively speaking

72 'Quite so', I hear an intelligent man say, 'Quite so, my dear fellow. At last I understand what you have explained in so much detail; namely that the increase in the number of marriages, which occurred from 1841 onwards, was, to a great extent, caused by the fact that from 1815 onwards, many more children were born than before, so that subsequently we have many more adults in the marriageable age groups. But I must admit that I don't quite see what ends this new way of looking at the thing really serves. I must also say that it seems to me that we don't get such an agreeable picture of human life from it either. I too, before today, have thought over the matter and I have the impression that I have found both a reasonable and acceptable explanation in the reflection that when God gives us good times, then it is easy for people to make a living, so more people can, with a good conscience, follow their heart's desire and establish a family. Besides, I have also thought that when, in one way or another, a certain improvidence of spirit comes to prevail in a country, then more people marry than otherwise would, including some who ought not to, at least not just then. According to your explanation, however, it appears that neither circumspection, nor improvidence has anything to do with it; that it is alone dependent upon whether many people or few come into the world. Human life does then actually come to be very much like a river that rises and falls according to the rain and the drought, which also happens to be the metaphor you yourself used.'

I can well understand these remarks and I shall devote this and the next chapter to answering them, providing, I hope, a convincing defence of my position and one which is consonant with the opinions on human life that I have just quoted.

73 First of all, I ought perhaps to draw attention to the fact that, in the introductory chapter, I prepared the reader by saying that enquiries carried out for this essay would lead us along a long and winding road before we could expect to reach our goal.

In the next place, I believe it would be a good idea if, now that we have come about half way and have conquered the worst hills, we pause to reflect on what might lie ahead in this enquiry and what end it might serve.

Think of a period of 20 years and imagine that in each one of the first ten years there were few new marriages, therefore few new families were established. But then, in the next ten years, suddenly the number was sharply increased. Some political economists consider a large number of marriages to be a perilous evil, or at least a critical state of affairs. Others believe that a small number of marriages is a bad sign. Whichever view is accepted – from the standpoint of either the reason or the result – in short, in whatever way the matter is interpreted and explained, it is still immediately obvious that the thing as a whole is at bottom concerned with the habits and circumstances of the people. Now it must be immediately apparent that the greater and more sudden that change in the course of the 20 years might be, the greater must be its importance, whether for good or for evil. Everywhere, therefore, those who want to understand the circumstances of the people also want to obtain reliable information about the founding of new marriages. This is of particular interest in a country where that change from one time to another, that rise and fall, that increase and decrease, has shown itself to be so unusually great.

Norway is just such a country.

74 I show this by grouping together all the relevant data that I have been able to find, namely the totals of newly established marriages in various countries and at various times. I arrange them firstly in periods of ten years and then, as in the previous chapter dealing with our five dioceses, I calculate by what percentage the number rises (+) or falls (−) between one ten-year period and the next (Table 19).

For every 100 couples who were joined together in marriage in the years 1801–10 in this country, there were 121 in the years 1811–21; that is, 21 per cent more. For every 100 couples married in the latter period, there were 110 in 1821–30; that is, 10 per cent more. For every 100 couples married in the years 1821–30 there were 96 in the years 1831–40; that is, 4 per cent fewer. For every 100 couples married in the years 1831–40, there were 124 in the years 1841–50; that is, 24 per cent more.

That then was the extent, according to the table, of the aforementioned rise and fall in the number of marriages in Norway. If one now compares this with the situation in other countries, one will see

Table 19. *Ten-yearly totals of marriages (their rise and fall expressed in percentage terms) in Norway, Sweden, Denmark, England and Wales, France and Prussia, 1801–50***

	Norway	Sweden	Denmark	England and Wales	France	Prussia
Period			*The actual number of marriages*			
1. 1801–10	65,306	198,390	78,908	832,151	?	?
2. 1811–20	78,712	216,199	92,603	910,426	?	?
3. 1821–30	86,639	228,968	95,475	1,052,095	2,476,204	1,076,268
4. 1831–40	82,914	215,060	97,796	1,189,628	2,661,532	1,248,215
5. 1841–50	103,096	240,420	107,156	1,355,492	2,803,300	1,401,385
Period			*Rise or fall from the one ten year period to the other*			
	%	%	%	%	%	%
From 1st to 2nd	+21	+9	+17	+9	?	?
From 2nd to 3rd	+10	+6	+3	+16	?	?
From 3rd to 4th	−4	−6	+2	+13	+7	+16
From 4th to 5th	+24	+12	+10	+14	+5	+12

* The totals for Norway and Sweden are taken from the official tables. The totals for Denmark, up to 1845, are taken from a general table in the English *Eighth Annual Report of the Registrar-General*; the rest from Danish tables. The totals for Prussia are drawn from Schubert's *Handbuch der allgem. Statskunde von Europa* as well as from Dr Dieterici's *Mittheilungen des statistischen Bureau's in Berlin*. The English table, referred to above, contained all the totals for England and France up to 1845; for the following five years I have used: for France, the annual communications of Moreau de Jonnes in *Annuaire de l'économie politique*; and for England, the German writer Horn's work which covers the population statistics of several states. It should be understood that under the designation 'England', Ireland and Scotland are not included. For Prussia and France and for most other states I deem it to be impossible to get lists of marriages right from the beginning of the century, and due to the fact that the many wars up to 1815 changed the frontiers of most states such totals from the earlier period would not be comparable with those from the later.

that the sharp increase in the number of marriages that took place in our country in the last ten years, was quite unusually large.[1]

There must, then, have been something unusual taking place in our country at that particular time. To discover what this was, is the same as to find the reasons for the marked increase in the number of marriages. On the other hand, by occupying ourselves with the investigation of the fluctuations in the number of marriages that have taken place in our country in the last generation, one is, at the same time, endeavouring to understand what marked changes have taken place in the lives of the people.

75 Yet one more circumstance gives this enquiry a special interest for us. In Table 19 we see that over the last half-century the experience, in this matter, of the three northernmost countries has been similar in that the number of marriages has risen sharply and fallen sharply. From the period 1801–10 to the period 1811–20, the number of marriages rose very markedly in Norway, Sweden and Denmark. From the period 1811–20 to the period 1821–30, the increase continued in all three countries, but it was a much weaker one. From the period 1821–30 to the period 1831–40, the number fell somewhat in Norway and Sweden and rose only a little in Denmark. From the period 1831–40 to the period 1841–50, the number of marriages again rose strongly in all three countries. The parallel is so marked that immediately one thinks that perhaps there has been a common cause and, should this supposition be confirmed, then a clear understanding of the matter as far as Norway is concerned would at the same time spread some light on the situation in the neighbouring nations.

76 With this I return to the alternative view that found a place at the beginning of this chapter and to which I have promised an answer.

The complaint is made against the explanation that I have given in the previous chapters, as to the reason for the marked increase in the number of marriages in recent times, that I have denied the humanity in human life. This is because, with my explanation, it looks as if human life runs on regardless; as if discretion and conscience or improvidence and vice (which are also human attributes) are of no consequence.

Let us set the views one against the other.

From the data in the tables, about which there is no dispute, we learn that in the years 1831–40 not quite 83,000 couples were married

---

[1] Now it will be understood why above (para. 68) I could describe the increase in the Throndhjem Diocese as great despite the fact that it was only 16 per cent and thus less than in the other dioceses.

in Norway, but that in the years 1841–50, there were over 103,000. 'Look', say some, 'look what an increase, what a happy increase. This total tells us so clearly what good times there have been in the country: a good and golden time for the agriculturalist and the fisherman – with flourishing trade and shipping – in short, with solid good fortune in all kinds of business, with rising living standards and encouraging prospects; a good and golden time, which caused even the most circumspect and careful to cease to be anxious of the perils involved in obtaining a livelihood, so that they ventured to establish families and by doing so increased the strength of the country.' I will not contradict the fact that the years 1841–50, with regard to these external circumstances, could be described as a happy time for Norway, though in the last half of the period considerable disturbances certainly occurred, about which we have already seen fit to talk (para. 25). I will not, as I said, set myself against the many well-informed men who are content to believe that in those years, taken as a whole, times were good. But what I will say is that the unusual rise in the number of new marriages must not be taken as proof of this.

'Look what an increase', say others, 'a threatening, indeed a frightening increase! No doubt, it could be considered somewhat harsh that people who cannot guarantee, at least to some extent, to provide for the regular maintenance of a family, should be forbidden by law to marry. But is it not necessary? Indeed, is it not for their own good? Round about us we see how hordes of people without reasonable prospects and with a most scandalous improvidence marry into wretchedness. It is reasonable to suppose that the increase in the number of such marriages must be very great for the country as a whole, for in my district and in the neighbouring districts and elsewhere, where I know people and have questioned them about the matter, the number of marriages has got quite out of hand. So much so that now one can say that, where before there was one family in a cottage, now there are two, if not three. Where will the food come from and the clothes for the children who will sprout forth? For times have not at all been so consistently good that we can take comfort merely in that thought.' I will not deny that improvidence can have been great. I have myself seen more than enough of it. But this I will say: the striking increase in the number of marriages cannot be explained by it.

77 Many circumstances in the years 1841–50 have acted as an invitation to people in this country to be happy, to set great store by the future and to arrange their domestic life after their heart's desire in a way which best serves the country's interest. But this same period has

also seen its difficulties, which have been an invitation to people to exercise a cautious prudence. The spirit of recklessness which always, as it were, lies in wait for the opportunity to penetrate into a man's soul, and into the lives of the people, has probably prevailed in the years 1841–50. Certain circumstances, however, have served as a beneficial counterbalance to it. Thus there have occurred many occasions for the humanity in human life to appear and to show its strength. The good nature in man has had its encouragement and its trials – his evil nature, its temptations and obstacles. My view is just that the reason for the marked increase in the number of marriages in the period 1841–50 is to be found neither in the higher living standard engendering optimism, nor in an increasing immorality or rudeness amongst the poor.

78 I began with the phrase, 'Many – but not relatively speaking'. What does it mean?

Take this example. Last year a field was sown with four bushels and bore forty. This year reclamation doubled the size of the field. Eight bushels were sown and it bore eighty or perhaps only seventy-two. Eighty or seventy-two is more than forty. That is immediately apparent. But reckoned in relation to the area of land employed and the amount of seed, one would have expected about as much. If I compare, therefore, this year's crop with last year's, I can say: a heavy crop, but not relatively speaking.

That is why I say: there were many marriages in total in the years 1841–50, but not many relatively speaking.

Would you not agree? If it was the case that the benefits of prosperity had aroused well-founded expectations in the people or nourished the spirit of recklessness, thus giving rise to a greater number of marriages than otherwise, then it must have happened that very many and certainly more of those who, so to speak, stood next in line to fill the ranks of the married, would have actually married as soon as it came to their turn, without hesitating or lingering, without considering the matter any longer. They who believe that must then say: 'Many, not only absolutely, but also relatively.'

The situation then is this. If the sentence: 'Many, not only absolutely, but also relatively' is correct, then the explanations given above are also correct. If on the other hand, my explanation is correct, the sentence 'Many – but not relatively speaking' must be true.

79 Throughout Europe, with the probable exception of Turkey and a few other countries, people have sought to discover by means of censuses and calculations whether there has been a relatively large or rela-

tively small number of marriages. Subsequently comparisons have been made between countries and between different periods in one and the same country. This type of investigation still forms a principal matter in the statistical writings which deal with population conditions.

The usual method of procedure is that one counts the number of marriages occurring over a year and then takes the total number of people. With these two totals one then finds the relationship between the number of marriages and the size of the population.

We shall do this as far as Norway is concerned. We know the census returns for the years 1801, 1815, 1825, 1835 and 1845 (Table 11). We also know the number of marriages for each period (Table 17). After this, it is a simple calculation to find out what the relationship was between them. This is presented in Table 20.

Table 20. *Number of marriages in Norway relative to the size of the population in the years around the census, 1801–45*

Population		Marriages		Each year one couple is married amongst the following number of people
Year	Number	Year	Number	
1801	883,038	1796–1805	68,230	129
1815	885,431	1811–20	78,712	112
1825	1,051,318	1821–30	86,639	121
1835	1,194,827	1831–40	82,914	144
1845	1,328,471	1841–50	103,096	129

80 What does this new table teach us? In the year 1835 – to stick to the later period which most concerns us – or, on average, in each of the ten years 1831–40, one must walk around the country until one has counted 144 people before one comes across one couple married in the course of the last twelve months. In the years 1841–50, on the other hand, one need not walk so far, for there occurred so many weddings in those years that one found a newly married couple for every 129 people. Therefore it is said that marriage has been more frequent, or relatively more frequent, in 1841–50 (1 couple for every 129 people) than in 1831–40 (1 for every 144).

Relatively more marriages in 1841–50 than in the preceding ten years? Has that opinion been proved correct, which said that the increase was brought about by the prosperity that made some people more hopeful, others more reckless?

81 The trouble is that the method of calculation adopted here is not

to be relied upon. Though often appearing in learned academic works, it has perhaps just as often obscured as enlightened. At all events it is the case here that it leads us away from the truth instead of towards it.

But why is this?

We must satisfy ourselves on the matter. And it won't cause us to rack our brains too much. Fundamentally the whole of this book deals not with complex numbers but with real human affairs, with well-known everyday events – with weddings. Mentally let us put ourselves in the middle of a wedding parlour. In some of our country districts there is still an old-fashioned custom. According to this each farm belongs to a *Bedelag* [*literally an invitation group – Ed.*], a certain part of the parish or specific group of farms, whose entire occupants, great and small, rich and poor, must be invited to weddings, christenings and funerals. Naturally, relatives and friends who live further away are invited along with the members of the *Bedelag*. Now probably in each of the years 1841–50 there were held, on average, 10,309 weddings, and we can conceive of the whole nation as related to these bridal couples – the whole country as members of a *Bedelag*, as neighbours of the wedding home. If no one was forgotten and no one failed to turn up, then a Norwegian wedding in these years would have consisted of 129 people; the bride and bridegroom being two and the guests 127. I venture to take the reader to such a wedding where in actual fact there were even more guests. Everybody is having a good time here. We cannot fail to enjoy seeing the gaiety of the young or be entertained when we share in the conversations of the old. Now and then during the course of the several days the wedding lasts, an attempt is made to give the company a more solemn character and we really feel ourselves to be part of the spirit of the occasion. Nevertheless, we do not forget what really brought us here. We would enquire whether weddings are frequent or not in the parish, whether the number of those that marry is greater or smaller, relatively speaking. With regard to this we must attend to what sort of people make up those 129. Now and then we let the eye wander slowly around the circle, and unobserved we are able to note down what we see and hear.

Look over there, a little apart from the bustle, sits a very old great-grandmother. Over there is the bridegroom's mother, also a widow, but still active and alert and zealously occupied with the entertaining. The bride's father and mother are also present. Over there on the bench, and round about, we notice several older people, mostly married men and their wives, among them several of the bridal couple's sisters and brothers. Some of the older people are already widowed. In the room where the dancing is taking place we find numerous young people gathered, and out in the entrance hall and in the farmyard a crowd of youngish boys and small girls tumble about. Even young babies are not lacking. Young wives from the neighbourhood have brought them along and take great pains to keep them quiet.

This was but a preliminary survey. We go further. We engage in conversations with our fellow guests. We seek in all possible ways to get a clear picture as to whether it is true or not that good times encourage people to marry, or whether perhaps the pressure of difficult times holds many people back. And we are able to question each individual quite bluntly, because it is plain ordinary Norwegian folk we are together with who know that in us they are dealing with honourable people. But we are not interested here in asking those who are already married what their impression is of the times and what they intend to do. Nor are we interested in questioning the old and decrepit. Quite naturally, too, we pass by the young children and the small boys and girls. The time has not come for them to think about such things. On the other hand, we could do well to speak with Halvor Host over there. He is a widower, but scarcely over 50 years old and he occupies a good farm. But don't question him yet. I know him as an honest but very quiet man, who pretty certainly will not wish to talk about this matter. But you can question his brother Ole Host. He is a cattle trader and has been for many years. He seems now to be about 45 years of age. Ask him what has kept him from marrying and he will answer in great detail that there are so many who try their hand at business now and that times are so difficult that it is a hazardous task to take upon oneself the duties of maintaining a wife and children. Then there is Ole Sletten, also probably over 40 years, obviously enough a crofter and therefore of that kind of people whom one very seldom meets in the unmarried state. But we should not consider him further. I know him as an enthusiastic marksman who till now has looked to nothing else than wandering over the mountains after reindeer. But over there is Sylfest Kvaale, a good-looking bachelor of perhaps 28, a farmer's son and non-commissioned officer. Question him – but you must question tactfully – and you will hear that he was not the eldest son. He, therefore, didn't have his father's farm to step into, and he got no great inheritance from his parents when they, against a fairly good allowance handed over the farm to their eldest son. If Sylfest got a farm today then he would readily have a wedding tomorrow. But it is not so easy to get a farm. Then there is Lars from the parsonage. He is known throughout the district as one of the most reliable of servants and for many years now the trusted retainer at the parsonage, from which he now takes his name. He is, I suppose, about 40 years old. Why is he still a bachelor? I wonder if it is from a love of cards, as we just now see him talking with the young players over there at the table. No, I know Lars very well and I know that it is only very occasionally that he touches cards. Nor does he play for high stakes now. That man, during his time in service, has laid away something for a rainy day. What then has been in his way? His father was a farmer who went down in the world. At an early age the boy was forced to look after himself and go into service. As a farmer's son, however, Lars was used to better things than most servant boys and he was not able to be content with just any sort of crofter's place. On top of this he has for many years now, since his father's death, expended not so small a share of his earnings in helping his old mother. All now depends on whether he is lucky with the cattle trading business he is thinking of starting and whether he can buy a small farm. I hope all will be well and I would be truly happy if I could happen to be in the neighbourhood and follow that man to church on his day of glory. Now this Lars made greater demands on life than most servant boys. But look, there goes another Lars across the floor; there sits Hans with his pipe; there Halvard takes to his mug; there sits Sigurd and nods. These and more young bachelors of 25–30 years or thereabouts don't demand much. They are servants, day-labourers, village shoemakers etc., and they would look upon it as a great event if they could get hold of a simple croft or a decent plot of land. But question them and you will get the same answer I got: at this time it is difficult to get hold of a piece of land and, as it is so expensive, it doesn't seem likely that one will become a crofter. 'But at this rate', perhaps you exclaim, 'there shouldn't be any more marriages in this parish.' That was not the meaning I intended to convey. Our handsome bridegroom is an example of the opposite. He has got himself, as you see, a worthy and respectable widow, who is in comfortable circumstances. And there are many other examples, for just in these last years the priest here in the parish has married an unusually large number of couples, a fact we can verify when we go into the parsonage and look at the parish registers. My intention was only to make you aware of the fact that if we want to know whether the number of marriages are many or few, relatively speaking, so that subsequently we can judge the people's circumstances and habits, we must go not to the children nor to the married people (because you cannot speak about the matter with them) but to the adult bachelors and spinsters, as well as to the widows and widowers who are not excessively old.

82 If we now, at one time in the period 1841–50, for example, in the course of the year from Midsummer day 1845 to Midsummer day 1846, could have gone round the entire country and been present at all the weddings and there found all the relatives and all the neighbours gathered together, then we would have been able to find and note down what the priests, during the course of the year, and the census at the New Year actually discovered and recorded.

Now will the work of the priests and the census be of some use. As a result of that work we can get a very good picture of what kind of people and how many of each kind there were present at a normal Norwegian wedding in this particular year, so long as we believe that the entire population took part in these family celebrations.

The number of weddings in that particular year was just 10 per cent of the 103,096 weddings that took place in the ten years 1841–50, that is, 10,309.

There were, it follows, an equal number of bridegrooms and brides. Of the people appearing in the census of 1845 there were:

1. Some who were not in a position to marry, or who could be kept out of the reckoning, namely:
   (i) Married (a) husbands   208,778
                 (b) wives   208,611[2]
   (ii) Children and young people under 20 years
                 (a) boys   292,480
                 (b) girls   286,509[3]
2. Those who were not prevented from marrying, at least not in the same way as the people above:
   (i)   (a) widowers   19,068
                 (b) widows   47,627
   (ii) Unmarried over 20 years of age:
                 (a) bachelors   131,867
                 (b) spinsters   133,438

---

[2] There must naturally have been the same number of wives as husbands; but perhaps on census day some men were away from home and were counted twice, both at the place where they had their home and at the place where they happened to be. In any case the enumerators have made a mistake, though fortunately not one of great importance.

[3] It is not quite true to regard all persons under the age of 20 as persons not to be considered as marriageable, for there are actually some people who marry under that age. But there are so exceptionally few boys who do so that, so far as they are concerned, the error is quite inconsiderable. It is a little greater so far as the girls are concerned; but here it is balanced by the common error of the enumerators, who often enter girls aged 19 or 20 in the over 20-year-old age group, something which I also noted in my essay *Om Dødeligheden i Norge (On Mortality in Norway)*, p. 22.

3. To this one adds a few people whom the census was not able to classify,[4] so that we do not know if they were married or not, but who, because they were so few, can without danger be set out of the reckoning. There were 40 males and 53 females: in all

	93

The grand total was therefore　　　　　　　　　1,328,471
which is the number given in Table 20.

If we imagine that these people, whom we spoke about before, were shared evenly amongst the 10,309 weddings, then the division would be about as follows (about because in this calculation there must be no fractions in the totals):

1. (i)		(a) husbands	20
		(b) wives	20
(ii)		(a) boys	28
		(b) girls	28
2. (i)		(a) widowers	2
		(b) widows	5
(ii)		(a) bachelors	13
		(b) spinsters	13

	Total	129

that is the bride and bridegroom, 2 and guests, 127.

83 This is about the same total as we found in Table 20. Now, however, we have learned that if we would properly investigate whether or not marriages are relatively few or relatively numerous, so that afterwards we can determine if the benefits of good times encourage people to marry or the pressures of hard times put off people from marrying, then we must only pay attention to those who belong to Class 2, namely the bachelors and spinsters in the adult age groups (over 20 years) as well as the widowers and widows. For all the rest must be left out of the reckoning. In 1845, or generally speaking in one of the years 1841–50, we must therefore think of the matter as follows. For every 2 widowers and 13 adult bachelors, one was a bridegroom. For every 5 widows and 13 adult spinsters, one was a bride. The others, 14 men and 17 women, were unmarried but were of marriageable age, so for that matter they were in a position to marry. But there were circumstances which caused them, either with or against their heart's desire, to put off marriage for the time being, or perhaps for ever. For the

---

[4] See *Om Dødeligheden i Norge* (On *Mortality in Norway*), n. 1, p. 20.

moment they must just sit and look at the one couple whose celebration they attended.

Here then is the true position: each year there was 1 bridegroom from amongst 2 widowers and 13 bachelors; each year 1 bride from amongst 5 widows and 13 spinsters.[5]

84 Now was this many, relatively speaking, or was it not?

If there were married each year, for 10 years, 1 person in 10, that would be the greatest imaginable rate. For then everyone would be married in the course of 10 years. But this situation can never actually occur. Some die during the 10 years, and overall there are usually one or two who prefer to remain permanently unmarried. The situation in the year 1845 must then be described as remarkable in itself.

But what we are concerned about here is to discover if the rate in 1845 was great or not, compared to that in 1825 and 1835. This we can ascertain from Table 21. It has been worked out in just the same way as has been explained above, except that I have been compelled to go into more detail and use not only whole numbers but also fractions.

85 The lesson which this table contains can be presented in the easiest way as follows.

At a normal wedding in this country in 1825 (and probably in each of the years 1821–30) we can imagine there were about 12 widowers and bachelors (12.2). Amongst them was one bridegroom. The remainder, the rest of that same 12, were probably, for the most part, people who certainly had the desire to raise a family, but what had happened to them was about the same as we heard from our friends at the wedding we described above: various circumstances came in the way so that they must delay marriage for at least a year.

In 1835 there were, besides a couple of widowers, whom as we noted before were mostly old men and therefore ought not really to concern us, 12 bachelors (to be exact 12.2). It seems, therefore, that the obstacles in the way of people wanting to get married had increased, as the total of those who did marry was relatively less than in 1825.

In 1845, finally, or in each of the years 1841–50, there were to the nearest whole number 13 (12.8) bachelors. That is more than in 1835.

---

[5] It would have been yet more accurate if we could have set out of reckoning all the widowers and widows who were already of that age (e.g. over 60 years) in which they seldom or never marry. In 1845 about three-quarters of them were over 50 years of age, and it was probably the same in 1835 and 1825. For these last-named census years, however, we lack evidence on this. Here, therefore, I limit myself to the remark that, when working with the earlier census years, we stick to the totals of bachelors and spinsters as the most numerous and most important class. See the following footnote.

Table 21. *The number of marriages relative to the number of*
marriageable men and women in Norway, 1825, 1835 and 1845

Year	The annual number of widowers and bachelors who married		The total number of widowers and bachelors	
			Widowers	*Bachelors*
1825	8,663.9			105,897
1835	8,291.4		16,625	100,835
1845	10,309.6		19,068	131,867
		Ratio		
1825	1	out of	12.2	
1835	1	out of 2.0	and	12.2
1845	1	out of 1.8	and	12.8

Year	The annual number of widows and spinsters who married		The total number of widows and spinsters	
			Widows	*Spinsters*
1825	8,663.9			138,297
1835	8,291.4		42,660	105,804
1845	10,309.6		47,627	133,438
		Ratio		
1825	1	out of	16.0	
1835	1	out of 5.1	and	12.8
1845	1	out of 4.6	and	12.9

We must then believe that such obstacles, which in 1835 led so many to go unmarried, still continued to operate and to a somewhat greater extent.

Relative to the number of bridegrooms, the number who failed to marry rose without interruption from 1825 to 1845.[6]

[6] The calculation is still not as exact as it could be. But for this one should have the following:
   1. The number of those who could marry, separated according to whether they were widowers, bachelors, widows or spinsters in the age groups 15–20, 20–30, 30–40, 40–50, 50–60, as well as
   2. The number of people in those different categories who actually married.
With these statistics one would then be able to calculate the marriage frequency in the different categories and at the different ages. Up to now there are very few countries in which such calculations are made, though in the Danish statistical tables of 1850 we do have a very fine example.

We have the details named under (2) above in annual returns made by the priests, but only from 1839 onwards (see Table 16 where those for the bachelors and spinsters are used).

In the main we also have the details named under (1) for the census years 1835 and 1845. For these years we have, first, all the people in the different age groups, secondly the married men and women as well as the widowers and widows in the different age groups. From this we can work out the number of bachelors and spinsters in the different age groups. But I have not been able to make any use

As for the women who married, there were more in 1825, fewer in 1835, and still fewer in 1845 relative to those who did not. Now some might say that the difference between 1835 and 1845 was not very great. That is probably true. But even so the extremely small difference here is enough to show the truth of the supposition, 'Many – but not relatively speaking'. For those who married in the period 1841–50 were at any rate not more, relatively speaking, than before, but rather fewer. So, therefore, the supposition I set up stands and the contrary supposition, 'Many in number and still more relatively', is not correct. But if this supposition is not correct, then the view that the unusually large increase in the number of marriages in 1841–50 was evidence of the benefits of prosperity or of an increase in recklessness, is not correct either.

86 Many in number, but not relatively. Rather fewer. With this is linked something else: namely that in the most recent period there were fewer bridegrooms and brides in the young ages, under 25 years, than we reckoned there should be (see Table 16, para. 61 where the matter is presented as an exception to an otherwise general rule). When a boy of say 24 years of age, who at the new year has perhaps half-decided to get married, sometime later during the year is induced to put off his wedding until the next year, he becomes 25 years old. If he then puts it off another year he reaches 26 before becoming a bridegroom. With this small illustration we have made it easier to understand the matter to which I must now draw attention. When, as we have seen in this present chapter, the number of marriages in this country in recent years has become relatively fewer than before, then we can put it down to the fact that people have delayed marriage, some probably for only a year, others for several years. So when they have finally married they have been older by some years than was the case earlier. The observation that in the most recent period there were so few bridal couples of a very young age, has already called forth the surmise that something must be going on to cause young people to delay marriage. This surmise is confirmed by what we have just learned, namely that there have been relatively few marriages in the period 1841–50. The fact that the two observations agree with one another, lends support to them both.

87 Many marriages in total, but not many relatively! The reason

of this information on the married and widowed, as the parish totals for 1835 are not aggregated at all, whilst those for 1845 are only done in part (see *census tables for 1845*, Introduction, p. x). As the original parish lists are still available this neglect can be made good, and certainly should be, at least for 1845, if we are to get the most out of the census.

for the markedly increased number of marriages in the period 1841–50, is not, therefore, the confidence inspired by prosperous times, nor is it recklessness (for that must first of all have shown itself in there being many relatively).

The result of the investigation presented in this chapter is this. The marked increase in the number of people in the marriageable age groups, the result of the great number of births from 1815 onwards which showed itself suddenly from 1841 onwards, I previously regarded as something that was to contribute to the rising number of marriages. It was one of several concurrent causes. It was something which must have played a certain role in producing the great number of marriages and therefore it was something that really ought not to be overlooked. It is now more correct to consider this circumstance (the great number of people in the marriageable age groups) as not one of the reasons but as the chief, the essential, the overriding reason. By the side of it the other things, which generally speaking elsewhere (e.g. in England) are regarded as the essential reasons (favourable contemporary conditions, good prospects etc.), sink to being subordinate circumstances, which have had some influence, but have not made much difference either way.

What in England is correctly regarded as the chief reason for the increase in the number of marriages (see para. 63) should here in Norway only be considered a secondary circumstance of small importance. Can such an opinion be reasonable? Yes, it can, in this matter, as in several others. Such another matter is the rise and fall of the sea against the beach. In England, the sea rises and falls regularly and to a very considerable extent. The same is also true along Norway's northerly coasts. Here in the Christiania Fjord, where the sea also sweeps in, the water level also rises and falls, but not so regularly and not to such an extent. This strong and regular movement, is the well-known ebb and flow of the tide. When, in the north of the country, the water level rises to its highest point, the fisherman knows that this is a common daily movement. He probably knows too that the reason for it lies in another globe, in the distant attractive power of the moon. When, on the other hand, the fisherman here in the Christiania Fjord notices, on some particular occasion, a somewhat higher water level than usual, he puts it down to a south-westerly storm out at sea. Storm and calm can undoubtedly, in the northern parts too, cause the tide now and then to be unusually high, or cause the ebb to sink back somewhat further than usual. But this is of less significance. The essential reason is quite different. The reverse also probably affects the ebb and flow in the Christiania Fjord, but its effect is too slight to be reckoned with. Whatever then is the chief reason in the one place, is an imperceptible secondary factor in the other. What in the one, so to speak, does everything, in the other does only a little either way.

In England, France, Prussia etc. it looks as if the essential reasons for the rising or falling number of marriages lie in contemporary events – the favourable or unfavourable circumstances of the time. It is, however, highly likely that after further investigation one would find that earlier events have also played their part; earlier events which have brought into the world, now a more numerous cohort of children, now a smaller one, so that later on the number of marriageable people is greater or smaller. But this has probably had less influence than those powerful contemporary events. In Norway, on the other hand, and in all probability also, though to a lesser degree, in Sweden and Denmark, there has in the last two or three generations been the marked peculiarity that it is just those earlier events, working at a distance, that have been overriding, whilst the contemporary changes of good and bad times, have, by comparison, exercised only a small and very temporary influence. In the Norway of this century, an extraordinarily strong ebb and flow has shown itself in the movement of the population, the regularity of which has only been disturbed slightly by contemporary events, the storm and the calm. In England and other countries the same ebb and flow has been so small that it has not up to now been perceptible.[7]

---

[7] In Nordland or Finmarken it would not be possible to travel a single day without noticing what the ebb and flow means. In the Christiania Fjord, on the other hand, one could spend a lifetime without thinking that there was such a thing. This example illustrates how it has come about that the statisticians of other countries have not noticed the condition we have discussed here, or, if they have come to think about it, have not given it any great weight. Earlier, in para. 63. I spoke about how in the works of foreign writers I had not found any hint of the opinion that an increase in the number of marriages at a certain date could be due to an increase in the number of marriageable people, in its turn, the result of an increase in the number of births at a certain earlier date. After this was written, and the whole of the preparatory work for this essay completed, I found a new and comprehensive work, which had in the meantime come into the University Library (*Bevölkerungswissenschaftliche Studien aus Belgien* by I. E. Horn, Leipzig, 1854). Here (vol. I, p. 223) the idea is presented, though it is argued that it is not correct. According to this writer if we find the 'marriage frequency', i.e. whether marriages are many or few relative to the whole population (including even married people and small children), then we should find, as we did in Table 20, that it was greater in 1841–50 than in 1831–40. From this we should conclude that as times had been so much better in the period 1841–50, this alone had caused an increase in the number of marriages that was greater than that in several of Europe's most flourishing countries (para. 74). The increase had then nothing to do with the fact that the number of marriageable people in the 20–30-year age group had fallen in 1835 and risen so markedly in 1845 (Table 17), nor that of these marriageable people at least as many, relatively speaking, as before

must remain unmarried (Table 21). The good times in 1841–50 (at any rate the truly very unusual times) should then have resulted in the fact that of those who were old enough to marry and yet still remained unmarried (for there is no point in talking about the others), there were *more* than before who did actually marry and *at least as many* as before who were compelled to put off marriage. Thus whereas before, of 100 marriageable persons, let us say 80 married and 20 remained unmarried, so now from 100 such persons we should have 90 marrying and still 20 remained unmarried! In the same way one could show, after observing the water in the Christiania Fjord, that there was no ebb and flow in the north of Norway, and that, therefore, there was nothing in the assertion that the moon influenced the movement of the sea.

9

Competition for bread

88 When we compare the total of those who went into regular marriages with the total of those who became the fathers and mothers of illegitimate children, we find that the latter rose even more markedly in the years 1841–50 than did the former. At the same time (1841–50), the number of criminal offences increased in like manner to an alarming extent. It was in about these years too that the great emigration to America aroused both astonishment and sorrow. It was also the case that at that time more and more people, especially those in poor circumstances, moved from district to district within the kingdom, in search of a livelihood. If one looks away from the past three or four years and recalls the situation then, one has to admit that it was more often the case that the worker had to look for work than that the employer had to look for men, and that it was not so seldom that unemployment prevailed. In 1845, a new poor law was introduced. During the next five years the complaint was heard, perhaps more than ever before in this generation, of rising poor rates. That mortality in the period 1841–50, though rather less than in the period 1831–40, was nevertheless greater than in the period 1821–30, is in itself a somewhat dubious indication of the health and vigour of the people. For after the long period of peace and progress one would have expected it to have been lower. The men or the authorities who have to find people to fill, not only the major public offices, but all sorts of minor and quite poorly paid posts, have probably never seen so many candidates as just at that particular time. Up till then we had indulged in an almost unalloyed pleasure at 'Norway's splendour'. Came there reports of strife and unrest in other countries, we sang with confidence:

> The rocky peak which bears the pine,
> is the free city of cheerful souls.
> The tumult of the world below
> reaches not my heavenly abode.

But the Workers' Agitation of 1848 was not the work of 'cheerful souls'. It was 'the world's tumult' which rather violently brought home to us the fact that our 'free city' could also be threatened.[1]

In these same years, 1841–50, the number of marriages rose from not quite 83,000, which it was in 1831–40, to over 103,000; an increase so great that we do not find its equal in any other country; not in England, France, Prussia, Denmark or Sweden (para. 74).

89 If we, as many have done, would explain this increase as a result of the fact that improvidence had gained the upper hand, that poor people married as soon as the natural desire was there, then how should we explain the still greater increase in the number of illegitimate births? For does not this rather run counter to the theory of reckless or improvident marriages?

Or if we, as others have done, would explain the increase in the number of marriages as the result of the country's great prosperity which made it so unusually easy for people to find a livelihood, how should we make sense of the fact that at the same time there were so many who turned to crime, that so often one heard of unemployment and helplessness, that so many were compelled to migrate, that feelings between workers and employers were so bitter that the tension was at breaking point?

I do not understand how these things can be reconciled without the help of the clue about marriages, contained in the phrase 'Many – but not relatively speaking'.

90 The idea behind this phrase must be developed further, so I put

---

[1] Some of this can be substantiated with figures. The number of illegitimate births, not including the still-born, was:

1816–20: 12,136
1821–25: 12,670
1826–30: 12,614
1831–35: 12,111
1836–40: 12,017
1841–45: 15,731
1846–50: 17,479

The number of persons who were punished in the civil and criminal courts for breaking the law were:

1836–40: 6,993
1841–45: 8,782
1846–50: 11,616

The emigration to America, which in 1841–45 scarcely amounted to 5,000 persons: see *Femaars Beretningen om Rigets Økonomiske Tilstand 1841–45 (Five Year Account of Economic Conditions in the Kingdom 1841–45)*, p. xxxi, and which it is fairly certain earlier had been even less, rose in 1846–50 to 10,779.

On mortality in the years 1821–30, 1831–40 and 1841–50 see my essay *Om Dødeligheden i Norge (On Mortality in Norway)*, Ch. 9.

On internal migration see the same essay, p. 126.

up this new thought. That which caused the marriages in the period
1841–50 to be so many in number also caused them to be so few relatively speaking.

The number of young people in the marriageable age groups increased suddenly and markedly in the years 1841–50. It was this circumstance which caused the marriages to be so numerous and yet so
few relatively.

Perhaps these sentences appear somewhat strange and difficult to
grasp. But we should not make the thing more difficult than it is. We
should remember that it is purely human and domestic matters that
we are dealing with here; matters too that, quite recently, we have
lived to see and take part in, nearly every one of us.

91 We are accustomed to regarding marriage and employment as
two things that belong together. It is true that some have employment
and yet do not think about marrying. On the other hand it can happen
that some go and publish the banns and have the wedding etc. without
having any means of employment. But those cases are so very rare that
for the time being we can discount them, leaving intact the expression
'so many jobs – just so many marriages'.

In this discourse on employment and marriage, it is only the men I
am thinking of and only those who are marrying for the first time, i.e.
bachelors. For when a widower takes his second or third wife, he is, for
the most part, only continuing his old household which was based on
an earlier employment.

When a ship's captain dies, or a new ship is launched, and a ship's
mate then gets a command, he has what he calls his livelihood. The
ship's boy perhaps does so when he is engaged as an able seaman. The
candidate for office can get an appointment either in a newly established post, or when an existing office-holder retires. This is his livelihood.

So too is it when the clerk becomes a parish constable or when the
trainee teacher gets a permanent position. When a farmer becomes old
and gives up his farm, it may happen that the eldest son keeps the
whole of it, and this then yields only one livelihood as before. But it
may also be the case that the farm, whilst it was held by the previous
occupant, was improved and extended, or that his various sons have a
mind to undertake such work themselves. So they share it between them
and thus make several farms. And if everything goes according to
expectations several livelihoods come out of the one that was before. A
servant-boy can get from his master the place of a crofter who has
recently died. He can also get a place, intended for a crofter, marked

out in the forest, put a house on it, and then begin to break the fields and clear the meadows roundabout. In either case he hopes to have found a livelihood for himself. The village shoemaker who, on the death of his master, makes sure of the work in the houses where the latter, year in and year out, had attended to the occupants' boots and shoes, in a way takes over a predecessor's livelihood. If, on the other hand, the tailor who recently came home to the parish, with new tricks and new methods, wins for himself most of the best customers of an older and more old-fashioned tailor, we could say that he, in a way, shares another's livelihood. Finally, the mechanic who fits up a workshop and provides people with new and useful instruments which no one knew about before, creates for himself a new livelihood.

Now from such examples we could say that livelihoods are in part inherited or taken over from an earlier generation and in part created from new things by new men who stand out from the new generation.

92 If the population of a country grows fairly steadily over a long period of time, increasing only slightly from year to year, then one would always have somewhat more people in the one year than in the immediately preceding one, arriving at the age at which they must look for a livelihood. But the majority would be in the lucky circumstance of being able to take over either their father's or some other predecessor's profession or livelihood. Only the few who, in each year, were in excess of this number must show themselves lively and seek out a new position. But since they, as we have said, would only be few in number, it would not be difficult for them. One might also say that it is to the country's great advantage that there are always a certain number of young and energetic men over and above the number needed to take over the previous generation's occupations and work. For, since these 'surplus' people, as we might call them, are forced to exert themselves – without overtaxing themselves – in order to enlarge the existing means of earning a livelihood, or even with great skill and shrewdness open up new ones, then is the wealth of the country made more abundant.

93 How has it been in our country in recent years?

In the years 1821–30 there were 86,639 marriages. That then, was the number of men who married. But of these I would guess there were only 86 bachelors in every 100,[2] that is, 74,509. In 1831–40 there were 82,914 men married and the number of bachelors amongst these was by the same calculation, 71,306. Finally, in the years 1841–50 the

---

[2] That was the position in the years 1841–45, and in this there is usually no great change from one time to another.

number of men getting married was 103,096 and the number of bachelors amongst them was, by an actual count, 90,131.

We assume that more or less all of these people had got a job before they married though there must have been great differences in the manner in which they got it. In the period 1831–40 the number of marriages was small, as against that of the previous decade. This accords with the remarkable fact that in 1835 there were few people in the 20–30-year age group, that is, the age at which most people both look for a livelihood and think about establishing a family. But with the number so small, it is reasonable to suppose that the majority obtained employment and a fixed position by a kind of inheritance from an earlier generation, so that only the minority were obliged to open up new opportunities. The ability and industry of the rising generation of energetic young men was, for the most part, occupied in keeping in operation the activities of the existing population. There was neither the need nor the numbers for any particular expansion.

94 It was otherwise, however, in 1841–50. Now there were 90,000 who married and who we assume had found employment; 90,000 as against 71,000 in the previous decade, an increase which must be described as extraordinary. How did this come about? How could it have been possible? Whatever the reason, the fact itself is remarkable. But it would have been absolutely inconceivable had we not known that at the same time, from 1835–45, the number of young men in the 20–30-year age group had increased from 82,809 to 116,295. Of this latter number we can assume that 83,000 had the same access to employment as that same number had in 1831–40, mostly by inheritance from forebears or by only a slight expansion of earlier businesses involving no great difficulties. But, as we have seen, the number of jobs found in this way was not the same as the number actually procured, namely 90,000. Where, we ask, did the rest come from? The answer is, out of the energy, the hard work of those 116,000 young men; from the exertions of ship's carpenters and of sailors; of fishermen, farm labourers and foresters; of handworkers, shop assistants; of physicians, clerks, schoolteachers etc.; altogether an army of about 33,000 men all in their most energetic years. The farm or business of their parents fell not into their hands. But they themselves had hands to work with and what have they not been able to do? They had ambition and courage in their breasts, brains in their heads and what new things have they not been able to find?

Many a stretch of wasteland that had waited since primeval times now got to know the mattock and the spade. Many a stream that till then had seen its power go to waste now got its mill to drive. Many a full-grown pine that before must have stood in fear of languishing away in its lonely wood was driven out and laid down in the keel of a new ship. The countless shoals of herring and cod which come so faithfully to our shores, now found a livelier reception from a greater number of hands. Even special laws and a special police force were needed to prevent friction amongst the host of fishermen on the sea. During the whole time that I have travelled through the countryside, farmers have told me about the considerable expansion of agriculture that has taken place in recent times and when I have then asked at about what time this expansion can be said to have begun, it seems it goes back to about the period we are dealing with here, the time when that radical generation, brought into the world from 1815 onwards, began to take control of agriculture and everything else. These more enterprising farmers have set more people to work. Besides, many a young, strong labourer has been forced to do road work (and, with a will quite different from anything known in earlier days, has worked himself up in the world) so as to make the roads more passable for this bustling generation. Who, indeed, can reckon how people knew how to open fresh ways? Look at the student of 1841. First he diligently acquired the knowledge that a graduate must have. Then if, for example, he was a theologian or a medical man, he sought out his work place and, as energetically as ever, cleared the dead wood until the people round about understood that it was worth money to put their children into the school of such a capable teacher or pay for medical assistance from such a clever doctor.

95 Certainly the period 1841–50 is a very remarkable one in our business annals. All the old branches of industry pushed forth vigorous shoots and new branches emerged by their side. The rich crown of this tree of industry soon arched over the happy roof of many a new family and its lively growth promised golden fruit.

But all growth takes time. So we may ask: was the growth fast enough? The fruits, drawn from the earth by the skill and labour of the people – naturally assisted, sometimes more, sometimes less, by the sun and the rain, and by God who causes all things to grow – should satisfy hunger and gratify need. The fruits' abundance – was it enough? Put more plainly: was it the case that the many in need of a livelihood, actually got one?

Certain writers in political economy continually assert and stress the proposition that in old states, in countries where people have lived and worked for a long time, nearly all the fertile spots and all other fruitful places of work are fully occupied. It is therefore difficult for the growth of the economy to keep in step with the continued increase in the size of the population. Thus there always arises the danger of over-population. Now this proposition is combated by another, which I myself prefer to believe, namely that with morality and industry it will be man's fortune, under normal conditions, to see business extended to the extent of the needs of the expanding population. But I think I may say here, without expecting to be contradicted, that there are always great difficulties in the realization of this expectation when that population growth occurs unevenly, as it were, by fits and starts. But this is just what happened with that part of the population of Norway we are dealing with here, namely that young, energetic group seeking a livelihood, seeking a subsistence; that group of 20–30-year-old men, newly come to adulthood; such an important age, fit for so much good, disposed to so much evil. Here we no longer have those steady 'normal conditions'. The marked increase in this group of the population in the years 1841–50 was anything but normal. Rightly the question is raised: does what applies under normal conditions apply here, namely that the adult population knows how to acquire adequate employment?

96 In any case competition must arise. It is not difficult to understand that when several people apply themselves to one and the same goal (the acquisition of a particular job) and summon up all their energy in order to achieve it, then we are pretty certain to get strong competition. Even so this could be only for the good since because of it many skills are roused to useful activity which otherwise would have lain dormant. But one can also imagine that the competition would become so fierce that it became a competition for bread.

97 Competition for bread? If you would really have an idea of what that can mean then go along in that small boat, watch them hoist the sail and keep it set no matter what might happen so as finally to beat the other pilot boat yonder and so be the first to come alongside the brig, from which they can perhaps (for it is by no means a certainty) get the job of piloting it in. Or visit a crofter clearing his land. Follow him out to the newly broken field where, with his crowbar, he is engaged in raising great heavy stones and watch him take such a grip that he turns dizzy. Put yourself in his place when the landlord and the tradesman come to him so that they each might take their share of the profit of his labour; the one for the rent of the land, and the other for the price of his crowbar, which was bought on credit.

Competition for bread! Just as the gulls in their noisy, shrieking thousands flock together over the herring shoals along Karmoen's wintry shore, so do the people. Thousands of small fishing boats have come from afar, the majority flimsily built of pine, though there are some stronger ones made of oak which threaten to run the others aground, out there near the breakers, around the outermost rocks. Further in, along the narrow bays and creeks, lie scores of the larger seining boats, fitted out by wealthier men. Each is manned by a sein master and perhaps twenty crew – poor labourers, whose sole hope depends upon its earnings, of which each man has a certain prescribed percentage. Think of the hour when the herring shoal makes for such a bay? The sailing boats lie in a row along the shore, one on the outside, the rest inside. Each boat's company wants to be the first to stretch a net across the bay. But none of the many crews will labour in vain before they are certain that the precious shoal is inside so it can be caught and held by the net. So the sein masters scan the ocean, straining every nerve, watching for the right moment. The crew too, hold themselves constantly in readiness, the net ready to be cast, the oars on the water ready to go at their leader's signal. Truly it matters, for only one party will be the winner. The rest will, perhaps in this one hour, lose the last hope of any profit whatsoever from this year's fishing; a profit which during the year had been reckoned so much upon.

Competition for bread! The shoemaker's bench, the student's chamber, the merchant's office, the field, the sea, Norway's thousands of small valleys, nooks and crannies, fjords and sounds, even the mines deep inside the mountains – here are the witnesses, who can tell all that they see?

98 There must have been competition for bread in our country. That we can see for ourselves by looking at certain prominent and unmistakable features of the country's situation, which, sad to say, point to it.

If there is competition for bread there will be many who are worsted in the contest. They will either never see themselves in a permanent position with an adequate income, or at any rate will not do so as quickly as they reasonably could have wished. Such people are obliged to postpone the establishment of a family either for a time or for ever. In 1841–50 this was the situation for many people. For the marriages, though many in total, were yet few relative to the number of those who were of the right age and who no doubt wanted to marry. This is something which our investigations in previous chapters have brought home to us.

If there is competition for bread, there are many who lack employment and for that reason dare not think about marriage. If they need only postpone it a year or two then the danger arises that they will fall into the temptation of living an immoral life and if they do then misfortune will occur more frequently. And it has occurred in our country in the years 1841–50: as a proof of this, witness the sharply increased total of illegitimate births at that time.

If there is competition for bread, many find themselves disappointed of their expectations. It can happen quickly then that now one, now another, allows himself to be overcome by despair and, one step further, becoming indifferent to his own honour, violates the rights of others. Something like that, one is bound to believe, occurred in our land in just those years 1841–50, since the number of those whom one has been compelled to punish for theft and other crimes has risen so considerably.

If there is competition for bread, many at one and the same time must apply for work and look for sustenance. Then will work be cheap and bread dear. And if it goes far unemployment will occur. But in the period with which we are dealing the evil of unemployment was felt not so seldom.

If there is competition for bread, then the amount of employment will fall short of what is required; and naturally, if many find themselves in this situation, they will eventually come to regard their underemployment as liberal enough, will rest content with it and will, quite probably, still establish a family even in their straitened circumstances. But such families run the risk, when a crowd of children appears or some misfortune occurs, of sinking into poverty and helplessness: and in the period 1841–50 there has been a strong complaint of increased poor rates, especially for young families.

If there is competition for bread, one finds oneself cramped. The prospects seem gloomy both for the present generation and for the growing one. So it is reasonable that people should think about going to another country where conditions are said to be more roomy and where there is a better living to be had: to emigrate – the young people for their own sake and the parents for their children's. The period 1841–50 was the time of emigration to America.

If there is competition for bread, the crush lasts for a long time and the pain is felt acutely. Then can the masses become impatient, the mood of the less-happy part of the population become bitter, the tension between the different parties and interests in society threaten to burst. Think of the crofter yonder on the land that he has newly reclaimed suddenly pushing the crowbar into the ground, as if to bid defiance to the landlord and the tradesman. He turns grudgingly towards them when they come to demand their due. But it was in this way that the Workers' Agitation was ignited towards the end of our period – from 1848 onwards. Great numbers, feeling their need and trusting to their strength, almost forgot right and duty, law and order – in which society's, and we would hope, not least, the sufferer's comfort and strength lies.[3]

99 So the years 1841–50 were a time of progress and a time of distress. Society and the State made great advances in strength and prosperity, greater than ever before; but many individuals experienced distress and need, worse than had ever occurred. We have looked at the light and the dark features on the face of the country. Everything fits into this explanation of the situation as a whole: from 1841 onwards there suddenly appeared an extraordinarily numerous cohort aged 20–30 years. This injection of extra energy increased business activity to a considerable extent, as we were made aware by the fact that a much greater number of people than ever procured employment and saw themselves in a position to establish a family. But it also produced distress. Many saw their hopes dashed. We are made aware of this by the fact that many people, though they were of the right age, were nevertheless obliged to refrain from establishing a family (the marriages, rightly enough, were, therefore, many in number but not many

---

[3] There was distress in the land in 1841–50; that was one thing. Another was that, amongst a by no means small part of the working class, a way of thought that was, in itself, good and to be wished for, came to be articulated. It was felt that as the sons of a free people they were not getting their share of the blessings of society. More was wanted of education, freedom and well-being. That at any rate is my opinion of the Workers' Agitation. But, on the other hand, one should not devote so much time to this matter without also remembering briefly what in all probability it was that caused the movement to die down so quickly, that turned dissatisfaction into peace and quiet. It was the new, good, free social order. The majority of the members of the Workers' Agitation belonged to that cohort of children, those new citizens of the world, who were the first to be greeted with the promise of freedom by the Constitution of 1814. In 1841–50 they were grown men, demanding the fulfilment of that promise. And it was fulfilled to an extent that is seldom seen in this world. Every intelligent man must admit that in our country we were free, that the spirit of freedom and the principal of equality prevailed here to a degree that in general is rarely to be seen. Every man was free to use his talents to serve both himself and society. He was free to move from place to place, to choose his own livelihood, to utilize every favourable opportunity that providence offered him. He had great freedom to present his views (either by himself or together with others), to publish his complaints, to demand his rights. His energies were not restrained, his aspirations were not clipped back. And it was in just this that society's best defence lay, against all the dangers of that undoubtedly perilous time. Freedom stood its test then.

relatively) and with that several other moral and civil misfortunes resulted on a scale worse than before.

100 Do I now then deny entirely that the good conditions, which indeed on the whole are admitted to have prevailed in the period 1841–50, had any share in causing the number of marriages to be so great? Not at all. But I must explain myself as follows: the good conditions helped to reduce the distress of the period and the number of people who were forced to delay their marriage.

Do I maintain that recklessness did not make any difference either way; that it did not bring considerable numbers to marry at an early age without due regard to their economic circumstances? No, I do not. But I do say this. Had this kind of recklessness not been so great then in all probability the calamity of a high illegitimacy rate would have been even greater.

The chief reason lies in the remarkable, in other countries probably unheard of circumstance, that the crowd of young men and women in the 20–30-year age group increased so markedly from 1841 onwards, that while the total of men in 1835 was 82,809 and of women 89,539, in 1845 they were respectively 116,295 and 122,971, an increase therefore of 40 per cent (33,486) in the case of men and of 37 per cent (33,432) in that of women.

Prosperity or recklessness, here as always, have been of some, indeed, of great significance; but by the side of the former circumstance, even this much has been small.

101 'Forgive me,' says a well-affected man, 'this is still a new way of looking at the matter and I confess that I do not quite understand it. At any rate there is something that does not seem to fit. Up to now you have spoken about the years 1841–50. But what about 1851–55? The former are looked upon as good years and even more so the latter. For some time now one has not heard so many complaints about the poor rates; the desire to emigrate seems also for the most part to have ended; the Workers' Agitation too is quiet and there is a somewhat greater need for workers than for work. In this same period too the number of marriages has increased. Have we not here, then, proof that good times, more than all the other reasons put together, can increase the number of marriages and that this increase can rightly be regarded as testimony to good conditions in the country?'

With regard to this one must note the following:

(i) The number of marriages has not increased very much in the recent, especially favourable, years. The yearly number, calculated as an average, was (see Table 1):

1821–25: 8,816
1826–30: 8,512 a decrease of 3.5%
1831–35: 8,447 a decrease of 0.8%
1836–40: 8,136 a decrease of 3.7%
1841–45: 10,118 an increase of 24.4%
1846–50: 10,501 an increase of 3.8%
1851–54: 11,122 an increase of 5.9%

The years 1841–45 were more favourable, much more favourable, than the five preceding ones and many people have said that the particularly sharp increase in the number of marriages (over 24 per cent) was the result of this. By comparison 1846–50 was an unfavourable period (dearth in 1847); the potato blight; in no year any really good corn harvest; standstill in business after the February Revolution); and for all that there was a great number of marriages, and not so small an increase over the previous period of about 4 per cent. The years 1851–54 are acknowledged by all as being ones of unusually good fortune (fine, in part excellent corn harvests; a rapid sale of Norway's products abroad; fabulously high freight rates); and still the increase did not reach 6 per cent. Had the opinion been correct that the influence of good times was overriding, then one would have expected a decrease in the number of marriages in the period 1846–50 and a very sharp increase in 1851–54, as in the years 1841–45. But that didn't happen.

(ii) The increase in the number of marriages which took place in 1851–54 is scarcely greater than what one would just about have expected in view of the increase that, in all probability, again took place in the number of people in the working and marriageable age groups. That this is reasonable, one will understand when one considers that the persons who in the current year, in 1855, are in the 20–30-year age group, are for the most part the survivors of the cohort born in the years 1826–35, a cohort that was considerably greater than that of 1816–25, from which came those who, in 1845, were in the 20–30-year age group (see lists of births in Table 12). After 1815, we see a new generation step forward. Its magnitude was apparent in the years 1816–25, but it grew somewhat more in the years 1826–35. From 1841 onwards, that same cohort stepped forth into the adult age groups, firstly with great force in the years 1841–50 and then in greater numbers still from 1851 onwards. Essentially for that reason, then, the number of marriages rose in the years 1841–50, and not unnaturally continued to do so up to 1855. If I should venture a prediction, it must be that the number of marriages will still rise somewhat further in the years 1856–60, but then the rise will stop and there may even be a fall in the years 1861–65.[4]

(iii) The change for the better that has occurred with the disappearance of unemployment and other setbacks in recent years (1851–55) ought not to be attributed purely to the good conditions then prevailing. One recalls that it is now fifteen years since 1841, when, according to my view, the pressure, and with it the resulting difficulties, began. Even with average conditions, it could well be expected that the situation would become better after such a long period of time. This year rich crops grow in many fields that were first cleared and cultivated after 1841. Today many hands find employment in factories whose owners first got the capital to build after 1841. Indeed many seamen this year have work on ships which were built last year with the money that an old ship had brought its owners in the previous year. In short, the unusual activity, indeed strain, which thousands of new men were called upon to face during the years 1841–50 has now begun to bear the expected fruit. The early difficulties of that new and numerous generation have now been overcome. That generation whose conduct and fortune at that particular time we have now looked at, the men of 1841, have harvested the fruit of their labours and still need helpers and helpers' helpers in order to manage the harvest properly. So now only good can come from the fact that the number of young people in the 20–30-year age group is a little larger today than in 1845.

---

[4] From the Norwegian Life-Table for 1821–50: see *Om Dødeligheden i Norge* (*On Mortality in Norway*), p. 34, I am able to reckon about how many of the children born in the years 1826–35 can be assumed to have reached the age of 20–30 years, and so be alive in the year 1855. I can also arrive at the same figure, through knowing how many were 10–20 years old in 1845, by using a method, which is the reverse of the one given above in the footnote to paragraph 65. The number of males was:

by the first method: 129,268
by the second method: 128,959

These more or less equal totals would fairly certainly have been close to the actual one if there had not been so much emigration at this time. However it is unlikely that emigration was so great that the number of males in the 20–30-year age group in 1855 would not have been much greater than in 1845. However, we shall fairly soon get to know the truth of this matter as a result of the census at the beginning of next year.

By the same kind of calculation it may be assumed that the number will be somewhat less in the years 1861–65. It is, therefore, reasonable to assume that the want of workers, from which our industry for the time being suffers, will continue, except in so far as one can make do with boys of 15–20 years, whose number by that time will have increased (see para. 102). [In 1855 there were 123,164 men aged 20–30 years and in 1865, 123,068. The mean number of marriages per annum in the years 1856–60 was 11,663 and in the years 1861–65 it was 11,386. – Ed.]

102 The storm has abated in the land. It was to be expected that this would occur. Heaven's blessings in recent years have caused it to happen somewhat faster and more completely than would otherwise have been the case. But anyone with a short memory can peruse the poor lists; count the number of those sentenced to hard labour on the fortresses in order to support their illegitimate children; visit the prisons and the workhouses for vagrants; look around the hovels in the suburbs or on the outskirts of country parishes; and he will find many living witnesses still from the time when there was competition for bread, when economically and morally it went ill with many people. On that account one should be forbearing in one's judgements, mild in one's usage and ready to help. And there is one thing still that we should consider. Now, in 1855, the country is governed by a greatly increased stock of men between the ages of 30 and 40 years – that numerous crowd in fact whom we met in 1845 in the 20–30-year age group. Governed, I said, for while it is the barely adult men of 20–30 years who with their youthful vigour work themselves and society forward, it is the 30–40-year-olds, seated on the councils and in parliament, and in the chair of honour in the growing family circle, who make the law of the land and raise families with principles. These men now watch a numerous flock of children grow up, a flock greater than at any time before. One knows that from 1841 onwards, when the number of marriages increased so suddenly and so markedly, the number of births also increased, just as suddenly and on the same scale (see Table 12). Here again, as it were, is a new generation. The eldest of them, in 1855, are fifteen years old; and many priests this year have certainly noticed that they have had an unusual number of children to confirm. We could count the years to when they will be adults. So if nothing quite out of the ordinary occurs in the meantime to bring about an extraordinary mortality or an extraordinary emigration, then in the years 1866–75 once more a considerably increased number of people will appear in the 20–30 age group. Like their fathers in the period 1841–50 they will look about for employment and think about getting married. But what will happen if there should be many who find their natural desires disappointed; if many fall into despondency and immorality, into lewdness and drunkenness and theft; if many are obliged to marry in straitened circumstances, so exposing themselves to the risk of impoverishment and to being a charge on the poor rate; if many should find it too confined here at home and be glad to turn their back on their fatherland? What indeed if the mood of the people is bitter and society becomes exposed to the misfortune of civil strife? That will depend not only upon the year's temperature (i.e. a good or bad harvest) or upon stock exchange dealings (lively or flat business) or upon such other things as human sagacity can affect only slightly. Essentially it will be founded upon the morality and ability that young people take with them from their childhood days and upon the freedom that is allowed, the encouragement that is given to young men, to use their great energy in opening up new fields for themselves. But this in turn will be founded upon the wisdom and care with which the fathers of the country and the fathers of its families today and tomorrow watch over the education and the upbringing of the rising generation; on the breadth of vision with which they evolve the institutions of a free state; in their patriotism, so that they put up with want and sacrifice in order to encourage the growth of industry so as to accommodate the needs of the future. Here is not the place to talk about what shall be done. Only I feel that on occasion it helps to clarify what is needed, if we set clearly before our eyes the fact that in a certain, not too distant, future – a future, indeed, in which most of us hope to share – a markedly increased need will arise, a need that demands something of moment to be done now.[5] Indeed there is reason to expect that the need will grow. For it is a characteristic of life in a free and civilized society that one enlarges one's ideas as to what one needs in order to live a happy life and subsequently one's desires accord with this. One wants more and more of the things that can embellish one's surroundings and improve one's existence. One's expectations of life, as we say, increase day by day, just as fast as the means to satisfy them increases. In the continual change of ideas and customs lies the excitement of life in a civilized society and its great danger. In the future that we spoke of, much that now appears good or bad will be seen in a different light. Many opinions that are now approved of will probably by then have become old-fashioned. Things we do not now understand will then command men's thoughts. But one change can be expected, indeed to a certain extent must be desired and hoped for, namely that one's expectations of life will be greater then than now.

103 The expectations of life! Here I mention something that I had in mind already at an earlier stage when I spoke about employment. Employment is an economic matter, but human life is not regulated by

[5] I can mention something that should be done. At first I thought to use it in a metaphorical way, so as to clarify the meaning of the present generation's great obligations towards the coming one; but it is more than a metaphor, it is a serious matter. The farmers in Gudbrandsdalen must not destroy all the wood on their mountain slopes, but if at all possible plant new trees so that their successors will not want firing and timber and perhaps suffer other, even greater misfortunes.

economic matters alone, but also by moral considerations, by inner feelings, and by inclinations. To these belong one's expectations of life and, because these are sometimes greater, sometimes less, it is, as was indicated, not quite accurate to say: so many jobs – so many marriages. If the expectations of life in one period are greater than in an earlier one, then there will be many who delay marriage because they believe they still do not command enough. If our expectations of life were formerly less, then fairly certainly there were more who, contented with very little, married in frugal, indeed even in miserable circumstances. Now I have already frequently referred to the opinion that a primary reason for the great increase in the number of marriages in the years 1841–50 should be sought in a growing recklessness on the part of a great section of the nation regarding the amount of thought given to domestic needs. Thus poor people married without means, indeed, without even a reasonable prospect of providing for a family. What this opinion really amounts to is that the expectations of life within that particular circle of people had diminished.

However, I put forward some new arguments against this opinion. First, it is certainly the case that the expectations of life have actually increased amongst the upper classes, in which I reckon the farmers as against their servants and crofters. As evidence of this I could mention the very general complaint of a growing luxury, a complaint I am still rather inclined to reject than to share. Rather I would refer to that which I confidently dare to call the general practice of daily life in the 'better' houses, as we call them, where stress is laid on greater comfort and on providing children with a better education. I am of the opinion that it is as natural as it is fortunate that such signs should show themselves especially amongst the radical generation, as I have called it, which from 1815 onwards was drawn into life; the generation which, in its younger days, breathed in the ideas and feelings of freedom and independence and so from 1841 onwards, sought to create a home and a family life that would in some measure accord with its expectations. And secondly, those of our fellow citizens who stand on a somewhat lower level of well-being and breeding – the lower classes, as we call them – what reason can one give for the opinion that the same nobler spirit has not entered here also? There is indeed in our country no yawning abyss between the two classes. The man of property, the master, lives in the parlour; the worker, the servant, is in the room next door. Only a thin wall divides them, with a wide door in between that is continually opening and closing. The ideas, the opinions, the habits move easily from the one room to the other.

104 Or will some people still assert that while the expectations of life have risen in the upper classes and resulted in a limitation in the number of marriages, the complete reverse has occurred amongst the lower classes, so that many people, instead of following the example of the former, have, in the period 1841–50, struck out into all kinds of recklessness? Now this can be answered not just by guesses and generalized assertions, but with figures. First, we have figures which force us to assume that whilst the number of people in the marriageable age groups rose very markedly in the years 1841–50 this increase took place more amongst the workers than amongst the propertied classes.[6] Secondly, we have presented figures in this book which show that new marriages in the same period, many though they were in total, were still not many relatively, so that rather more people than before put off their marriage. Would anyone then still say that working-class people, in their recklessness, were prompted into marrying earlier and more frequently than before? If this were so then the number of marriages in the poorer classes should have increased to an extraordinary extent for two reasons: first, because there were so many people in this class and secondly because these same people were said to be so quick to marry as compared to the members of the propertied classes, who must, therefore, have balanced this increase by a more than doubled limitation on marriage. But, in this case, the limitation on marriage on the part of the propertied classes would have had to be much greater than our daily experience of the matter leads us to believe. Probably, then, the truth of the matter is this: the expectations of life have risen and have contributed to limiting the frequency of marriages in Norwegian society, both in the labouring and propertied classes, though most probably to a greater extent in the latter.[7]

I have also, as one has seen, a strong suspicion that, after 1841, there have been somewhat more frequent examples of newly married people

[6] See essay *Om Dødeligheden i Norge* (*On Mortality in Norway*), p. 146.

[7] Naturally this is something quite different from the fact that marriages, as we shall see later, amongst the working class are somewhat more frequent than amongst the propertied class. But fairly certainly this was the case in earlier times also, and so it in no way runs counter to the view that recent times have seen limitations on marriage in the working class too.

It was with reference to this point in particular, that I said, in the opening chapter, that in the course of this essay we would certainly come to feel the want of several pieces of evidence. The statistical tables do not give us details of marriages for the differing stations of life separately and the facts which I have privately collected, and which I shall give in the following chapter, do not allow us to compare the present with the past. For that reason it is earnestly to be wished that someone in the future would consider getting hold of this kind of information.

of the working class being compelled to accept poor relief within a short time of their marriage. Yet this occurred together with other events testifying to the straitened circumstances in the country. So that it is at any rate as correct to blame it upon the times of scarcity as upon the moral conditions prevailing.[8]

105 If we cast an eye back upon the hills and valleys through which our investigation has wandered, there lies before us a series of observations. The number of marriages rose suddenly and sharply in the period 1841–50 both in the kingdom and each of the five dioceses (Chapters 2 and 3). The reason for this lies in the marked increase in the number of children born after 1815 and the resulting increase in the number of young people in the marriageable age groups from 1841 onwards (Chapters 4, 5, 6 and 7). Though in turn this led to a greater total of new marriages, relatively speaking there were not so many (Chapter 8). It was probably the case that this great number of young people led to increased economic activity from which many found employment and so were in a position to raise a family. But this same multitude also entailed distress within the country, under which many who were less lucky were obliged to put off marriage, and besides put up with a number of other great hardships that followed. These were at their worst in the early years, but by the period 1851–55 it seems the initial difficulties were overcome. The primary reason for the more notable changes in marriage which we have witnessed in recent years lies therefore in the internal composition of the population, itself a product of the earlier population change. By the side of this such circumstances as are otherwise looked upon as being the essential reasons – changes in the external conditions at the time and in the moral position – must be considered to have exercised only a subordinate influence. So far has the present chapter brought us.

106 Favourable conditions, by aiding the efforts of those engaged in winning a livelihood, always contribute to increasing the number of new marriages. But favourable circumstances also usually have the effect that mortality in a country becomes less. This was the case in Norway in 1841–50 in comparison with 1831–40. But if mortality falls, then it is less likely that older tradesmen die; less likely, therefore, that younger men can take over their occupations. Here then those same

---

[8] At a time when employment opportunities are good a 22-year-old boy with nothing more than his two bare hands, marries, and he comes through pretty well. At a difficult time, such a boy puts off his marriage till he is 26 years old, and sometime after gets into difficulties. Who would venture to say that this is evidence of a greater recklessness on the part of the latter?

favourable circumstances make it somewhat more difficult for people
to establish a family. Good times mean an increase in prosperity, which
leads to the development of ideas about what belongs to a happy family
life and to an increase in what one expects of life. And this development limits the frequency of new marriages. Here too then is an effect
and a counter-effect. In good times the expectations of life are com-
monly increased and this would, as we have said, limit the frequency
of marriages and their number; but it happens in good times too that
a greater amount of the prosperity is collected into single hands, so
that a greater crowd of workers collect together about the single man
of property and the business manager. In other words the working
class grows greatly in numbers by comparison with the propertied
class. But if greater and greater demands are made on life by the
working class also (and marriages are always more frequent within this
class) then we can understand why one and the same circumstance can
work both towards an increase and a decrease in the number of marriages.

What, relating to the present matter and so far as Norway is concerned during the last generation, I have called subordinate circumstances, are circumstances which are not only able to change very fast
and therefore for the most part exercise only a short-lived influence, but
are also such that in many ways they cut across each other, working in
opposite directions and so cancelling out each other's effects.

These subordinate circumstances ought naturally to be an object for
attentive investigation. But to attempt to determine their influence
accurately, or to investigate thoroughly the relationship beween cause
and effect here, would be as if a naturalist should take compasses, a foot
rule, a lead and a watch and then, placing himself by a rapidly running
river, try by all kinds of measurement and reckoning to discover cause
and effect in the river's course; to discover why the thousands of drops
and wavelets move this way and that; to apprehend why the currents
and counter-currents sometimes move quickly, sometimes slowly, now
upward now downward, sometimes here to the side, sometimes foaming
and frothing, now flowing evenly, sweeping along smoothly. Such a
task is naturally endless. Instead of finding the rule and order that is
sought for, the eye of the investigator is bewildered by the many
tumbling shapes.

107 But stand somewhat further back from that same river, so that
the eye is no longer entrapped by the many details but gets a better
view of the whole. Then can one discover the rule and the order. Do
you not agree that often you have looked this way with wonder at the

river's course and with delight have dwelled upon the beautiful sight?
What is it? All indeed is incessant movement, but in the middle of that
movement, which would tear the glance with it, your eye holds fast to
certain images and figures, so formed and finely drawn that you wish
for a pencil to draw them with, and yet so light and airy that you
despair of ever doing so; shapes which seem to assume solid forms and
remain stationary before your gaze, whilst the waves that formed them
continually disappear. It is the regularity in the windings and whirlings
of the waves. From second to second, from hour to hour, they remain
unchanging – appearing identical to the eye. But come again some days
or weeks after. Then can it happen that you do not find the same old
pictures again, but instead completely new ones. For in the meantime,
due to rain or a thaw in the mountains, the river has risen strongly.
The movement is rapid, the waves hurry past in great haste, the whirl-
pools and eddies hurl themselves around, everything twists and turns
and swings even faster, in a shorter course, in narrower circles. The
stream of human life, of the life of society, is, you will find, the same.
You find that to be so in different ways – in the situation regarding
marriages, for example. For a long time the stream flows quietly and
regularly with each year a new generation of young people rising up
into the marriageable ages. Pay attention and you will find a certain
relationship, a certain law as to the number and frequency of the marriages. This applies, more or less unchanged, from one time to another,
from year to year, although the people concerned in each new year are
different. But then a time comes and that quite suddenly, when the
stream, as it were, swells, when particularly numerous generations, one
year's cohort after another, without a break, rise up into the marriageable ages. Pay attention and immediately you will find a changed
situation. There is distress. All hurry towards the same goal, but it
becomes more difficult to reach that goal. Meet and separate quickly –
quickly – that is the watchword. Even associations for life are less
lasting. Marriages, put off to a later age so there is less of mortal life
left, are quickly dissolved by death. A shining wave, colliding violently
in the rapid stream becomes, as it were, crushed and broken and dis-
solves into scum. Now displaced, unable to make its own way, light and
will-less it is borne away on the backs of the other waves. In the same
way we must see in the human herd, in the irresistible stream of social
life, now one, now another, whose power and independence were destroyed; human beings who in moral and civil respects went to the bottom, so that, from the day of their misfortune, they live a life without
joy, a burden on the rest of society. So the population stream in our

country is like a river, whose source lies in the immense snow masses on the high mountains. The mild warmth of a spring rain can quickly pierce the masses of snow and in time the river will foam and froth. Sometimes it rises above its narrow bed and floods the country around, loading the fields and meadows with sand and stone, tearing out bridges and embankments. We are accustomed to rivers of this sort in our land. Little by little we shall probably succeed in dredging and widening the river beds, in making solid brick-built bridges and embankments so that flooding will occur less frequently and the danger for coming generations will become less and less. Here we might liken society's growth to the swift course of the swollen river, with morality, education and industriousness as society's piers.

10

Differences in the country districts

108 'In your opening chapter you spoke of the widely held opinion that, in recent times, the number of reckless marriages had increased. Against this you set your own, somewhat contrary view, namely that the situation was not so bad and indeed that it was changing for the better. Now the fact is that for a long time I have belonged to those who support the former opinion. However, when I discovered that you were putting forward as full an explanation as possible on this so-important matter, I determined to go through it, point by point, and patiently I have held out till now.

'I won't deny that your explanation could be correct. But in saying that I do not yet admit that my view was altogether wrong. The point is that, whilst your figures and calculations relate to the country as a whole, my experiences and reflections apply to the single district in which I live. I now admit that, so far as this aspect of the people's life is concerned, there has been a change for the better in the country as a whole. I also admit that some of your remarks have caused me to see one or two things here in my own district in a different and, as it were, less critical light than before. Unfortunately, despite all this, I still say that recklessness in the setting up of marriages and, as a result, impoverishment and other misfortunes, are evils, which in recent years have increased here in my neighbourhood; a circumstance which could well be an unfortunate exception when compared to the rest of the country.' Such an objection will perhaps be made and I can well believe that it could be wholly justified.

Indeed by this objection we are reminded of something that is of the greatest importance for anyone who sets in train well-founded investigations into one or other aspect of the life of the people, namely that there is a great difference between one part of the country and another, a difference which makes the work of the investigator that much more difficult, and yet at the same time gives it a heightened interest.

109 The resident of the capital city and the country dweller, the agriculturalists of Hedemarken or Indherred, the shepherds in the high valleys of Østerdalen, the fishermen of Lofoten, the seamen and pilots in the outports from Lindesnaes to Hvaløerne, the miners of Røros and the sawmasters, sawmill workers or lumbermen at the Sarpsborg Falls – there we have people whose upbringing, customs, opinions, occupations, expectations and circumstances are very different, one from another.

In what does this diversity lie? Of what does that particularity and individuality consist that makes the people of one district different from those of another?

In a country such as Norway, with its considerable variations in natural conditions, it is likely that the work of the people will be extremely varied. But it is upon the means of earning a living that one's daily routine and domestic circumstances depend. From them are formed certain customs and ways of living. All this influences, little by little, one's entire personality, bodily health and mental development. Even the features of the face itself soon get their own stamp and the mind develops its own special strength and direction.

These external circumstances together with man's own inner drives go to make up the particular character of each district's population. Whilst, for the country as a whole, common social arrangements aim at promoting education, welfare and good morals in all districts in the same way, the general arrangements are implemented in different ways by the men of each individual district and as a result there gradually develops in the small society of the district a totality of ideas and opinions which can in many ways diverge from that of neighbouring districts. Or just as world history gives us examples of individual men who, to a marked degree, have been able to influence the thinking and customs of a whole nation, I believe it may well be the case that, by a careful search, we could find many examples of the fact that gifted people, even though of a lowly social position, have contributed much in the small circle of the individual district to giving the prevailing habits and opinions a new direction, sometimes for the better, sometimes for the worse.

So human nature can adapt and mould itself to external factors. It would seem, indeed, that the population of each district was created for the neighbourhood in which it is set to live and work. To the degree that people are influenced by the customs and habits that prevail we may often excuse even great personal failings by noting that such and such was a child of his time. But besides the influence of the time and place, there is also another circumstance that has undoubtedly contributed to produce that diversity between the people of many districts which we are now able to observe in our country; a circumstance, the reason for which lies outside our country's borders and is lost in the obscurity of an earlier time. I refer to what our historians believe they have discovered, namely that our country, from the beginning, was occupied by different races. Each race, although probably related and for the most part forming one nation, brought with them from their original home their own character, planting it where they settled, where it took root. Now one could well be of the opinion that, after the passing of so many centuries, those original racial differences must have been obliterated. But examples from other countries (and examples based on statistical evidence such as the extent that different kinds of crime reveal different temperaments) have shown that the original folk-nature can persist for an exceedingly long time. It may be that the difference in bodily form, mental quality and habit, which one can find by even a cursory examination, for example between the populations in the mountain districts of Valders and Gudbrandsdalen, can be put down to having stemmed from those remote times.

110 People's natures can, therefore, differ from one district to another. That there actually are such differences is well enough known. Indeed this matter is one of the most favoured topics of conversation. Travel from town to town along the whole of the Norwegian coast and everywhere you will hear how the people in the one town amuse themselves by passing comment on certain peculiarities of their neighbour's habits and customs. Travel from district to district and you will not fail to hear the common people practise their wit at their neighbour's expense. Usually opinions on a people's manners and conduct is expressed in humorous and often very long stories. One derides a district's pettiness, is irritated over another's haughtiness, expresses oneself disdainfully at a third's thievishness. In Romerike, in Hedemarken and in Gudbrandsdalen, these judgements are presented in rhymes (no doubt coming from the distant past) which name all the parishes in the entire district and with their sharp and often appropriate comments have a fling at every single one of them.

But whether the people in a country parish are thievish or dirty or lazy etc. should not be merely an object of humour. The matter is too important since it concerns a people's civil and moral fortune or misfortune.

The great variety of rocks which provide the foundation of our country, of plants which bedeck the shore, the valley and the mountain, the great variety of birds and fish and all kinds of other animals, have for a long time attracted the attention of naturalists. All educated men are pleased for each new discovery which by their diligence enriches the world. Should not then the many differences in human life also be a worthy object of our attention? And could it not be described as useful if eventually we can understand them more completely and more confidently? Would it not be valuable for the lawgiver, the public official, indeed for every citizen who feels for his land or his parish and would readily contribute something to advance the good and to counter the evil that may show itself?

Here, as in every science, there is probably much that will remain a secret, that always will evade the searching eye. But the man who seeks usually finds and I am of the opinion that if we had facts regarding schools and education, crime, immorality and drunkenness, religion, population increase, social class (property owners and workers), business conditions, wealth and poverty, the physical form and state of health, domestic arrangements and social matters etc., etc.; if we, as I say, had reliable and possibly complete information of these things for each single parish, then we could compare them one with another. Then we might expect to be able to reveal much that is now hidden from us of the physical and mental situation of the Norwegian people. Connections between cause and effect would emerge which, for that practical activity which seeks to further the people's well-being, would present a very useful guide to finding the right means for reaching the best objective.[1]

111 How did I come to talk about all this? It was through the objection that there could perhaps be one or more parishes that were exceptions to the general rule that people in the marriageable ages now have a lower marriage frequency so that probably fewer reckless marriages

---

[1] Naturally I am not saying that those aspects of the life of the people mentioned here have not received attention in our country. Indeed Kraft's topographical and statistical work on Norway contains wonderful information, especially on economic conditions in the different parishes, and Ivar Aasen's linguistic works provide a most excellent guide to the study of the major and minor links between the people of the various districts. But it is just the rarity of the care and skill with which these works are executed that arouses an even greater desire that the many other matters concerning the living conditions of the country people might be studied in the same way. Taken on the whole, one will find that there is far more written about the remarkable things in the kingdom of Nature in our country, than about the different forms of human life. The continuous changes of these forms makes a sustained attention to them doubly necessary. Speaking of this I shall not refrain from expressing my opinion that provincial newspapers could and ought to contribute more than they have up till now, to enlighten us about the habits and circumstances of the people in the individual districts.

are established than used to be the case. If there were such exceptions, if in any individual district things were so bad that recklessness prevailed more and more, then there must be, on the one hand, specific reasons for it and, on the other, expected results. It would relate to the entire life of the community and it would be very instructive indeed to know precisely what this relationship was. If this evil prevailed in a community, then a proper knowledge of it would be of particular importance for all the men of the community whose vocation in life it is to work for morality and the well-being of the people.

There are a multitude of observations to be made about the state of the people with regard to marriage in the different communities. I shall, by way of example, name one. As is indeed well known, the majority of marriage compacts are concluded between bachelors and spinsters and usually between somewhat older bachelors and somewhat younger spinsters. But in individual districts one finds quite marked deviations from this. One district where an unusual number of bachelors marry widows is in Nordland and Finmarken, i.e. the Tromsø Diocese. Here the reason plainly lies in the unfortunate circumstance, which I dealt with at length in my earlier writing *Om Dødeligheden i Norge (On Mortality in Norway)*, that such a very large number of young men perish at sea and so many wives become widows at an early age. But there are other districts in our country where, year after year, unusually large numbers of marriages are established between bachelors and widows, without any such obvious external circumstances as the reason. Such districts are, for example, Ryfylke Deanery in comparison with the neighbouring districts; also Øvre Thelemarken's east and west mountain deaneries in comparison with the Nedre Thelemarken and Bamble deaneries. It is to be feared that the reason here is the same as in the last century that learned priest Strøm complained about in *Søndmørs Beskrivelse (Description of Søndmør)*, namely that 'young bachelors take old widows primarily to get a piece of land'. Mutual respect and personal inclination should be at the heart of the marriage pact. Marrying someone merely to get a plot of land is a narrow-minded calculation as culpable as the otherwise so-often-complained-about recklessness. The fact that very frequently, in individual parishes, marriages between bachelors and widows or between widowers and spinsters occur, can therefore be very suggestive of the prevailing ideas and circumstances of the district.

112 The understanding reader will not expect that I should give, in this essay, a full explanation of marriage conditions in each individual district of our country. For the work involved would be far too great.

On the other hand I dare to hope that the same understanding reader will approve of the fact that I devote some pages to the results of an enquiry that I have already carried out concerning marriage conditions in the different districts.

I think of the country as being divided into 53 districts which, for the most part, coincide with the deanery districts and which, therefore, can be indicated by the names of these.[2] From the lists drawn up each year by the priests, deans and bishops, I have taken the total of marriages for each district for the 20 years 1831–50. The information derived from these totals should be the starting point for further enquiries regarding individual parishes. But they also serve to support some of the views presented in the previous chapter and, therefore, an account of them has its rightful place in this present essay.

113 In paragraph 74 I showed how the number of marriages had increased from the 10 years 1831–40 to the 10 years 1841–50, namely:

in France	by	5%
in Prussia	by	12%
in England	by	14%
in Denmark	by	10%
in Sweden	by	12%
in Norway	by	24%

In a separate investigation of each of the 5 dioceses reported in paragraph 68, we found that this increase was:

in the Christiania Diocese	32%
in the Christiansand Diocese	18%
in the Bergen Diocese	19%
in the Throndhjem Diocese	16%
in the Tromsø Diocese	28%

Whether, therefore, we look either at Norway as a whole or at the individual dioceses, we cannot but be surprised at such a marked increase in the number of marriages in the years 1841–50 in our country by comparison with that in other countries.

But now we ask, did this unusual condition occur in each individual district of our country? Were there no exceptions?

The answer to this question is contained in Table 22, where I list all the deanery districts in the order they come in the country, moving from east to west and from south to north.

[2] The classification is just the same as the one I used in my essay *Om Dødeligheden i Norge (On Mortality in Norway)*, Chs. 12 and 13, and about which I gave a full explanation in app. 4 of the same essay.

114 The only district in the entire country where the total of marriages in 1841–50 was less than in 1831–40 was in the Lister Deanery. It is not difficult to guess the prime reason for this. In the period 1831–40 or in the majority of these years, the sild fisheries were unusually rich here. Living standards rose rapidly and expectations of life even more. Therefore many people were enticed from other parishes and here, as was shown everywhere, the benefits of prosperity caused unusual numbers to establish families. But at the changeover to the ten years 1841–50, the profitable sild fishing suddenly ceased. Instead of well-being and liveliness of spirit, there was great anxiety and alarm. As it became more difficult for people to find employment, so marriages occurred less frequently. But now, to a greater extent than before, the deanery districts of Stavanger and Karmsund came to benefit from the profitable fisheries and we find from Table 22 that, in these districts, the number of marriages rose to an unusual extent. So I dare to suggest that an accurate knowledge of business conditions in the entire country in the period 1831–40, as well as in the period 1841–50, would explain much of the differences between the districts shown in Table 22.

There is one thing to which I must draw attention. The country outside Norway where we found the greatest increase in the number of marriages in 1841–50 was England (14 per cent). Yet in Norway's 53 deanery districts there are 41 in which the increase was greater than this.

These 41 districts lie partly on the coast, partly inland; partly in the south and partly in the north. These 41 districts vary enormously in their economic activities, the fortunes of which, for many reasons, could be so very different. When the Hedemarken farmers get their barns, their bins and cribs well filled, Indherred perhaps has a year when the crops do not ripen. It can happen that when the timber trade goes well and brings life into Østerdalen's woods and Sarpsborg's saw-mills, the fishermen in Nordland get a poor price for their fish. It would indeed, therefore, be very remarkable if the economies of all 41 of Norway's 53 districts should have been so very much more prosperous in 1841–50 than in 1831–40 to the extent that one, on this ground alone, could explain the fact that the total of marriages rose more than in a booming England.

115 How then do I explain it? I have already done so. In the previous chapters I have pointed out that one must take regard, not only of the circumstances of the present, but also of those of earlier times. In the years preceding 1815, the country was at war. Many people must have delayed their marriages and the number of children born was

Table 22. *Percentage rise or fall in the number of marriages in the deaneries of Norway from 1831–40 to 1841–50*

No.	Name	Percentage	No.	Name	Percentage
1	Nedre Borgesyssel	+21	27	Stavanger	+49
2	Mellem Borgesyssel	+21	28	Karmsund	+51
3	Vestre Borgesyssel	+26	29	Ryfylke	+20
4	Øvre Borgesyssel	+24	30	Hardanger and Voss	+20
5	Nedre Romerike	+32	31	Søndhordland	+28
6	Christiania Diocese Deanery	+69	32	Bergen Diocese Deanery	+22
7	Øvre Romerike, Soløer and		33	Nordhordland	+24
	Odalen	+40	34	Ytre Sogn	+10
8	Østerdalen	+21	35	Indre Sogn	+3
9	Hedemarken	+36	36	Søndfjord	+15
10	Gudbrandsdalen	+42	37	Nordfjord	+17
11	Thoten and Valders	+38	38	Søndre Søndmør	+13
12	Hadeland, Ringerike and		39	Nordre Søndmør	+23
	Hallingdal	+28	40	Romsdal	+13
13	Kongsberg	+26	41	Nordmør	+19
14	Drammen	+32	42	Fosen	+23
15	Jarlsberg	+24	43	Throndhjem Diocese Deanery	+28
16	Laurvik	+24	44	Dalerne	+7
17	Nedre Thelemarken and Bamble	+14	45	Indherred	+16
18	Øvre Thelemarken	+16	46	Namdalen	+28
19	Østre Nedenaes	+14	47	Helgeland	+26
20	Vestre Nedenaes	+24	48	Salten	+19
21	Robygdelaget	+9	49	Lofoten and Vesteraalen	+39
22	Christiansand Diocese Deanery	+12	50	Senjen	+30
23	Mandal	+11	51	Tromsø	+38
24	Lister	−7	52	Vest Finmarken	+18
25	Dalerne	+12	53	Øst Finmarken	+38
26	Jaederen	+25			

smaller than usual. But the year 1815 brought peace and good times. Now unusually many new families were established and the flock of children increased markedly. From 1841 onwards these children reached the age of 25 years and, as a result, the number of people in the marriageable ages increased considerably, after which it was to be expected that the number of marriages would rise. What was expected, happened. That we have seen, so far as the entire kingdom is concerned (para. 65, Table 17) and we have seen it too in each of the dioceses (para. 67, Table 18). Now we learn that it is true also for the smaller deanery districts.

It is reasonable to assume that the misfortunes of war did not strike each individual district to the same extent. It is, therefore, also reasonable to assume that the result just described (the changeover from a smaller number of marriages in 1831–40 to a greater one in 1841–50) would not show itself to be equally great in each individual district. But the similarity is still so strong in the 53 districts that, with one exception, there is in all of them a rise in the number of marriages and in 41 districts that same rise is so strong that, by comparison with other countries, it can be described as exceptional. The general explanation I have given previously for the entire kingdom and for the five dioceses very probably, therefore, applies to the smaller districts too. It is thus difficult to deny that here again we have solid support for that explanation.

116 What we have given here can also be expressed like this. The movement of population in the majority of the districts is fairly similar, so that, for example, there have been few persons in the 20–30-year age group in the years 1831–40, many on the other hand in 1841–50. Had the movement of population been absolutely uniform in all districts then we would not need such an elaborate calculation as that which is used for the kingdom as a whole in paragraph 84 in order to find out whether people married more or less frequently. Then it would be enough to know the number of marriages and the size of the total population. Since the movement of population, as we have said, is not exactly the same everywhere, this simple method of calculating the frequency of marriage will not give an altogether accurate result. But still the similarity is, as we have seen, quite considerable in the majority of the districts, so we can assume that such an easy manner of calculation will bring us close to the truth. In the whole of Norway we find:

Population		Yearly number of marriages	
1835:	1,194,827	1831–40:	8,291
1845:	1,328,471	1841–50:	10,309
Average:	1,261,649	Average:	9,300

If I now compare these totals I discover that in the 20 years 1831–50, for each 10,000 people, about 74 couples were married (to be precise 73.7). This total is a measure of the marriage frequency in the period.

If I perform the same calculation for each deanery district, then I find that this total is sometimes somewhat smaller, sometimes a great deal larger than that for the kingdom as a whole. As a result I get the impression that the marriage frequency in some districts is somewhat smaller and in others somewhat greater; an 'impression', I say, and not something that is absolutely certain, since the calculation is not of the best, owing to the lack of requisite detail, as already explained.

The calculation is carried out in Table 23. Here the various columns contain the following information (from left to right):

1. The deanery districts numbered in such a way that we begin with the district where the figure for the marriage frequency is smallest
2. The district's name
3. The marriage frequency in 1831–50
4. The total indicating what percentage of the population in the course of the 10 years 1836–45 must be assumed to have been lost by out-migration (–), or gained by in-migration (+)[3]
5. The districts arranged according to the degree of out-migration and in-migration, so that the district where the population lost most by out-migration becomes no. 1 and the district with the greatest increase in population, due to in-migration, becomes no. 53.

Table 23. *The deaneries and dioceses of Norway ranked according to the number of marriages per 10,000 population in the years 1831–50 and the extent of in-migration and out-migration between the years 1845 and 1855*

1	2	3	4	5
1	Gudbrandsdalen	62.4	−7.1	1
2	Østerdalen	64.4	−2.2	19
3	Mandal	66.5	−3.1	11
4	Dalerne (Throndhjem Diocese)	68.1	−0.8	24
5	Bergen Diocese Deanery	69.6	+1.7	35
6	Østre Nedenaes	69.7	−0.8	23
7	Øvre Borgesyssel	69.8	−1.1	22
8	Øvre Romerike etc.	70.0	−2.3	18
9	Indre Sogn	70.1	−2.4	15
10	Hardanger and Voss	70.2	−5.6	3
11	Dalerne (Christiansand Diocese)	70.4	−5.3	4
12	Nedre Romerike	70.5	−2.7	14
13	Romsdal	70.9	+4.7	44
14	Vestre Nedenaes	71.0	+1.7	34
15	Namdal	71.2	+2.7	38
16	Vestre Borgesyssel	71.2	+4.1	43
17	Søndfjord	71.3	+1.0	32
18	Fosen	71.5	+4.1	42
19	Lister	71.6	−3.5	9
20	Nedre Thelemarken	72.0	−3.7	6
21	Kongsberg	72.1	−2.0	20
22	Indherred	72.1	+0.1	29
23	Mellem Borgesyssel	72.3	−3.0	13
24	Hedemarken	72.4	−3.1	12
25	Hadeland etc.	72.6	−4.2	5

[3] I have explained in my essay *Om Dødeligheden i Norge* (*On Mortality in Norway*) how I calculated the extent of in-migration and out-migration in the various districts in the years 1836–45, p. 126.

1	2	3	4	5
26	Thoten etc.	72.8	−2.0	21
27	Øvre Thelemarken	73.3	−6.4	2
28	Jaederen	73.5	−3.7	7
29	Christiansand Diocese Deanery	74.0	+0.4	30
30	Robygdelaget	74.4	−2.3	16
31	Nordmør	74.6	+5.7	46
32	Jarlsberg	74.7	+0.5	31
33	Throndhjem Diocese Deanery	74.7	+7.2	47
34	Laurvik	75.1	−0.6	27
35	Ytre Sogn	75.3	−3.6	8
36	Salten	75.6	+3.0	39
37	Nedre Borgesyssel	75.9	+1.7	36
38	Drammen	76.0	+2.1	37
39	Nordfjord	76.3	−0.2	28
40	Ryfylke	77.4	−3.2	10
41	Søndre Søndmør	77.4	−2.3	17
42	Helgeland	77.7	+1.4	33
43	Lofoten and Vesteraalen	79.8	+9.6	49
44	Søndhordland	80.0	−0.7	25
45	Nordre Søndmør	80.1	+3.8	41
46	Senjen	80.7	+3.6	40
47	Karmsund	80.7	+8.2	48
48	Tromsø	80.8	+5.2	45
49	Stavanger	80.9	+14.5	51
50	Nordhordland	82.9	−0.7	26
51	Christiania Diocese Deanery	89.3	+25.7	53
52	Øst Finmarken	94.2	+16.8	52
53	Vest Finmarken	107.6	+13.1	50
I	Throndhjem Diocese	71.4	+2.2	IV
II	Christiania Diocese	72.7	−0.5	III
III	Christiansand Diocese	73.2	−0.9	II
IV	Bergen Diocese	75.7	−0.9	I
V	Tromsø Diocese	81.3	+4.9	V
	Kingdom	73.7	+0.2	

117 When we compare the first and the last districts – Gudbrands-dalen no. 1 and Vest Finmarken no. 53 – we see that there is, by no means a small difference in the marriage frequencies. Amongst a population of 10,000 people in the period 1831–50 62 couples, on average, were married each year in Gudbrandsdalen, whereas in Vest Finmarken, on the other hand, there were 107.

But why have I also given the details of in-migration and out-migration? I beg to point out that in Gudbrandsdalen, where the marriage frequency was at its lowest in the period 1831–50, it so happened that more people moved away from the district than from anywhere else. That is to say, in the years that I know about, namely 1836–45, not less than 7 per cent of the population moved away, so that Gudbrandsdalen, in that respect also, was no. 1 of the entire 53 districts. In Vest Finmarken, on the other hand, the reverse was the case. There, people were moving in, and in such great numbers (13 per cent) that the district in this respect became one of the last in the series (no. 50), for there were only some few districts where in-migration was yet greater. It appears, therefore, that in the districts from which out-migration took place, fewer people married, and the reverse, that in the districts into which people moved, more married and established families.

And this applies not only to Gudbrandsdalen and Vest Finmarken, it applies to the majority of districts. In the first 28 districts in the table, the marriage frequency appears to have been less than in the entire kingdom (i.e. less than 73.7 per cent). But in the majority of these districts out-migration took place or there was only slight in-migration. In the last 25 districts in the table, on the other hand, the marriage frequency is seen to be greater than for the kingdom as a whole (i.e. greater than 73.7 per cent), and in the majority of these districts either in-migration took place or there was only a fairly slight out-migration.

118 This observation is by no means unimportant for one's assessment of the situation in the individual districts. I can believe, for example, indeed I have often heard it with my own ears, that people in Gudbrandsdalen complain of the great recklessness with which young and poor boys there go and get married. And there are many individual examples which are scandalous to a high degree and quite sufficient to warrant such a complaint. But I am of the opinion that one should take care in deciding whether the situation in this matter was unusually bad or whether that recklessness was very threatening. The true condition may be this. It is among the poor that a deep awareness has developed of the fact that it will probably not do to marry in such mean circumstances as the opportunities of the parish offer. A great number of the young people, therefore, have gone to seek employment in districts that are more fortunately placed than their own. At any rate, this observation agrees best with the figures we have found.[4]

---

[4] I myself believed this, so far as Gudbrandsdalen was concerned, long before I had the totals and calculations. In Gudbrandsdalen, farming is the only regular means of employment. But it is difficult for a poor man to buy land himself, and the increasing shortage of wood as well as the always-pressing need for pasture in the neighbourhood of the farms makes farmers little inclined to give up some of their more distant fields to crofters, or for men to clear. Under such conditions even very 'reckless fellows' find it problematic to establish families, and I have the impression, after repeated visits to the area, that such is the feeling even in the poorer classes. One soon notices also, after travelling amongst the people here, that a very large number of the young people, in particular of the crofter

It is natural for human beings, when they reach adulthood, to think
of marriage. It is natural too that they would fain stay at home. So
exceptional circumstances must occur before the young will do violence
to themselves and leave their native hearth. Now there are every year,
on average, several thousand couples who marry here in the country,
and if it could be proved that in recent years there were more stay-at-
homes who had not tried their luck outside their own districts, more
that is than in earlier times, then I would call this a serious state of
affairs, well tuned to sustain the opinion, maintained by many people,
that recklessness predominates; a recklessness whereby people only
follow their natural inclinations and marry without exerting themselves
further for employment etc. But our table now shows us how, in the
years 1836–45, there was much migration in the country; out-migration
from some districts, in-migration into others. We must necessarily
assume that, for the most part, this migration was of young, unmarried
people, who struck out to seek their livelihood. We find it reasonable to
suppose that eventually they settled down where they found the best
prospects. We presume that it was just people like this who contributed
to the fact that marriages were so frequent in the districts to which
they moved. And this confirms, what in another place I have demon-
strated, or at least shown to be likely,[5] namely, that this migration was
considerably more frequent in the years 1836–45 than in the earlier
period, 1826–35. All this leads us to the conclusion that the young
people of this country seem to have shown, in recent times, a heightened
eagerness to get to a position that could justify them establishing
families. This conclusion is in agreement with all the evidence which
earlier in this book I have presented against the dismal view that
youth's recklessness in this matter has been growing worse and worse.

119 Yet the fact that young people move away from one district and
marry in another is only one of the many circumstances which could
cause marriages to be less frequent in the one district or more frequent
in the other. First and foremost one should have the most reliable information possible as to which were the districts where marriages were
more frequent or less so, without regard to what the reasons for this
are. And so I use the data I spoke about in paragraph 116 (namely
population totals and the number of marriages) so as to calculate the

class, both girls and boys, have in recent times 'travelled away' mostly to the
north of the country, there to seek service or day-work.
    Many of them are now married and settled, and their migration has thus con-
tributed to the fact that the frequency of marriage is so low in Gudbrandsdalen,
but – as we also learn from the table – very high in most of the northern districts.
[5] See *Om Dødeligheden i Norge* (*On Mortality in Norway*), p. 126.

marriage frequency separately for the period 1831–40 and 1841–50.
The result of the calculation I give in Table 24 ,the columns of which
contain:

1 and 2. The number and name of the deanery districts in the same
order as in Table 23

3 and 4. The marriage frequency in the years 1831–40 and 1841–50 as
well as

5 and 6. The deanery districts ordered separately for 1831–40 and
1841–50, so that one begins with the district where the marriage
frequency was smallest.

Table 24. *The deaneries and dioceses of Norway ranked according to the
number of marriages per 10,000 population in the years 1831–40 and
1841–50*

1	2	3	4	5	6
*1	Gudbrandsdalen	52.6	71.8	1	8
*2	Østerdalen	61.3	67.2	3	2
*3	Mandal	65.6	67.3	9	3
*4	Dalerne (Throndhjem Diocese)	69.0	67.4	18	5
*5	Bergen Diocese Deanery	64.2	74.9	6	19
*6	Østre Nedenaes	69.7	69.8	22	6
*7	Øvre Borgesyssel	64.7	74.6	7	18
8	Øvre Romerike etc.	60.8	78.4	2	30
9	Indre Sogn	73.2	67.3	36	4
*10	Hardanger and Voss	65.7	74.4	11	17
*11	Dalerne (Christiansand Diocese)	68.8	72.0	17	9
12	Nedre Romerike	62.8	77.7	4	27
13	Romsdal	71.4	70.5	30	7
*14	Vestre Nedenaes	67.8	73.7	15	14
*15	Namdal	65.6	76.3	10	23
*16	Vestre Borgesyssel	69.2	72.8	19	11
17	Søndfjord	70.4	72.1	27	10
*18	Fosen	69.3	73.3	20	12
19	Lister	77.8	66.0	51	1
20	Nedre Thelemarken	69.9	74.0	24	15
*21	Kongsberg	66.5	77.3	13	26
22	Indherred	70.6	73.5	29	13
*23	Mellem Borgesyssel	67.4	77.0	14	25
24	Hedemarken	63.6	80.6	5	40
25	Hadeland etc.	66.3	78.5	12	32
26	Thoten and Valders	65.1	79.6	8	37
27	Øvre Thelemarken	70.2	76.3	25	24
28	Jaederen	68.1	78.5	16	31
29	Christiansand Diocese Deanery	72.9	75.0	34	20
30	Robygdelaget	75.4	74.3	46	16
31	Nordmør	73.3	75.7	39	21
**32	Jarlsberg	70.5	78.4	28	29
33	Throndhjem Diocese Deanery	69.4	79.5	21	36
**34	Laurvik	70.3	79.4	26	35

1	2	3	4	5	6
35	Ytre Sogn	74.3	76.2	42	22
**36	Salten	72.3	78.6	32	33
**37	Nedre Borgesyssel	73.3	78.2	38	28
38	Drammen	69.7	81.6	23	41
**39	Nordfjord	73.2	79.0	37	34
**40	Ryfylke	74.6	79.9	43	39
**41	Søndre Søndmør	75.0	79.7	44	38
**42	Helgeland	72.5	82.3	33	42
**43	Lofoten and Vesteraalen	71.8	86.7	31	47
**44	Søndhordland	74.2	85.2	41	46
**45	Nordre Søndmør	75.2	84.5	45	45
**46	Senjen	76.5	84.1	47	43
**47	Karmsund	73.1	86.7	35	48
**48	Tromsø	73.4	87.3	40	49
**49	Stavanger	76.6	84.2	48	44
**50	Nordhordland	77.2	88.1	50	50
**51	Christiania Diocese Deanery	76.9	98.7	49	51
**52	Øst Finmarken	87.6	99.6	52	52
**53	Vest Finmarken	106.8	108.3	53	53
I	Throndhjem Diocese	70.0	72.6	2	1
II	Christiania Diocese	65.9	78.5	1	3
III	Christiansand Diocese	71.5	74.7	3	2
IV	Bergen Diocese	72.2	78.9	4	4
V	Tromsø Diocese	76.3	85.8	5	5
	Kingdom	69.4	77.6		

120 From this table we learn, for example, that in Nordhordland (or Strile-land the marriage frequency in 1831–40 was 77.2 and that in 1841–50 it was 88.1. Thus in each of the two periods it was considerably higher than in most other districts, so that Nordhordland was at both times no. 50 in this series. It can therefore be supposed that in this district there are particular factors operating all the time which give rise to unusually large numbers of people getting married. On the other hand we find that in Gudbrandsdalen the marriage frequency was very small in both periods, so that the district was no. 1 in the years 1831–40 and no. 8 in the years 1841–50. But since in each of the two periods business conditions were quite different (partial scarcity and distress in some of the years 1831–40 and good times in most of the years 1841–50) and yet still the number of newly marrieds in Gudbrandsdalen was fairly small in comparison with most other districts, it is reasonable to suppose that there must be certain circumstances here which were not just of a temporary nature, but year after year acted as a check on people's inclination to marry.

We could classify the whole series of the 53 districts into two classes, namely the first 28 where the marriage frequency in the entire period

1831–50 was least and the last 25 where it was greatest. Of the first 28 it seems the majority (namely those marked *) belonged, in both individual periods (i.e. in 1831–40 and 1841–50), to that half of the districts where the marriage frequency was the lowest. Of the other 25 districts, it is seen that the majority (those marked * *) belonged, in both individual periods, to the other half of the districts where the marriage frequency was the highest. With individual exceptions, it has, then, in all probability, been the case that it is not merely temporary, more or less favourable circumstances, that have caused differences in the marriage frequency, but permanent ones.

What then are these circumstances? Rightly enough they can be certain peculiarities in the cultural position. When rudeness prevails, undoubtedly more young people marry recklessly and at an early age. When there is more education and circumspection amongst the people, more and more find themselves a firm position and tolerably certain prospects. But there are also many other circumstances which are at work here, e.g. the level of mortality. I have in another place[6] pointed out that where mortality is greater, marriages tend to be more frequent. This last-named circumstance ought to be attended to much more, as the greater or lesser mortality is not only an influence upon the actual situation, but also contributes to making calculations of marriage frequency, in the way that they are worked out in this chapter, less trustworthy.

121 But because these calculations, as often noted, are less reliable, and as I have not had the opportunity to collect the necessary details for every single one of the 53 districts, I append here an explanation of the marriage frequency in the five dioceses; an explanation which is built upon the same kind of information as lies at the base of the calculation in paragraph 84 with regard to the kingdom as a whole. This calculation is probably not the most perfect (see note, p. 87), but it does give a more reliable result. It differs mainly from that used up to now in this chapter in the fact that it only takes note of the persons who were of such an age and in such a position that they could marry, namely adult persons who were not already married (omitting, therefore, children and married people). For the sake of brevity I present the result of the calculation only so far as men are concerned. (Table 25).

This small and easily grasped table is extremely instructive. What I shall point out first is that it very clearly confirms the earlier presented proposition (para. 85) for the kingdom as a whole, namely that the marriage frequency has become less in recent times (that marriages

[6] *ibid.* p. 132.

Table 25. *Annual number of marriages per 1000 men aged 20 years and over (i.e. bachelors and widowers) in the kingdom and dioceses of Norway, by decade 1821–50*

Diocese	1821–30	1826–35	1831–40	1836–45	1841–50
Christiania	85	75	69	67	68
Christiansand	85	77	72	71	69
Bergen	80	78	73	70	72
Throndhjem	75	74	68	65	63
Tromsø	79	77	75	71	71
Kingdom	82	76	71	68	68

have become few relatively despite the fact they have become many in total). This shows itself to have been the case in every single one of the five dioceses. When, for example, in the Christiania Diocese in 1841–50, there were 68 marriages per 1,000 marriagable men, so is this a smaller number than in 1821–30, when there were 85. Next I must point out the fact that is as interesting as it is indisputable, that the marriage frequency in the Throndhjem Diocese is less than in any of the others, not only in a single short period, but in each of the 5 periods into which the 30 years from 1821 to 1850 are divided. How interesting this is and how important for a closer study of social conditions, one will understand if I but name a single circumstance which is most closely connected to marriage conditions, namely that through the whole of this century, that is, for as long as we have any knowledge of it, the misfortune of high illegitimacy rates has been much greater in Throndhjem than in any of the other dioceses.

122 In Chapter 3 I spoke about how this essay was, in part, occasioned by a lengthy stay in Gudbrandsdalen, the aim of which was to set in train investigations into certain social conditions. In the present chapter I have several times named Gudbrandsdalen as a district where marriages were not very frequent. This causes me to add a yet more exact picture of the district, one which is produced by the same kind of detailed calculation as in Table 25.

Of 1,000 marriageable persons, that is, bachelors over 20 years as well as widowers, there were married annually in each of the after-named periods:

1821–30	1826–35	1831–40	1836–45	1841–50
85	72	57	57	63

In the five years 1836–40 there occurred a series of bad years in several districts of Opland and not least in Gudbrandsdalen; bad years so serious that 'love gifts' had to be collected in the surrounding districts in order to help the needy. To this fortunately temporary circumstance must probably be attributed the fact that the marriage frequency showed itself to be so exceedingly small in the years 1831–40 and 1836–45. Nevertheless it is remarkable to see how small the average frequency is, both in the period 1826–35 and in the good times 1841–50, something one will find by comparing these figures with those in Table 25. This confirms the impression we already have that in recent years the frequency of marriage in Gudbrandsdalen has been very low.

I I

The upper and lower classes

123 In this book I dealt first of all with the differences in the number and frequency of marriages at various times during this century. Then I spoke of the differences that can be found in the various districts. But differences can also show themselves in a third direction, namely in the different ranks of society.[1]

The present essay is occasioned by the fear, voiced by many people, that in recent times there has been an extraordinary increase in reckless marriages. When, however, the frequency of such marriages is talked about as being a perilous evil, it is a certain class one has in mind – the lower class, the working class. An investigation of the matter ought not then to fail to take account of the habits and customs of this class.

I have not omitted this. I have shown that marriages in recent times have been less frequent in our country. The necessary conclusion from this is that circumspection, which is the opposite of recklessness, must have become greater, and have moved many to put off their marriages. And this conclusion – as I have expressly pointed out – must also apply to the working class, as this is the most numerous part of the nation (para. 103). I have, moreover, pointed out that marriages, on the whole, were less frequent in the districts from which out-migration took place and most frequent, on the other hand, in the districts into which people moved. It is fairly safe to assume here that it was in particular the young and unmarried members of the poorer classes who moved from place to place seeking regular employment. And as such migration has increased in recent years it is reasonable to see in that evidence of the fact that poor people were manifesting a rather greater effort to find such a position in which it could be considered justifiable for a man to raise a family (para. 118).

I am, however, in the fortunate position of being able to give more

---

[1] Moreover it could be enlightening to see what differences there may be in this matter, in the towns and in the countryside. But we must wait for this until the official population statistics supply the necessary facts.

evidence which should throw light on the question of marriage within the working class, or on the difference in this matter between the upper and lower classes.

124 There are probably not many things more likely to occupy the minds of today's philosopher than the differences in views, habits and conditions of life of the different ranks of society. Philosopher, did I say? The great and the erudite? No, take up any journalist's copy and you will get views and judgements about the different parties' interests and demands, about the virtues and merits or the wants and the faults of the higher and lower ranks of society. Listen to any conversation in everyday life and if it is a farmer you will soon hear his opinion of the conduct of the agricultural labourer or of the crofter class. Or if it is a crofter it is usually not long before you hear his view of the farming people's way of life and of doing business.

'Right now the farmers are so hard that it is not possible for poor people to live. My father paid five *dollars* for this place, so see if I get it under eight and even then the landlord has taken a good field from it. But that's what they are like.'

'There can't be anything but poverty for working people when they go and marry in foolishness as the greater part of them do. There is Halvor Nebben, as we call him, a real fool he is: not before he had stopped being on parish relief, well at any rate he had not been long enough in service to get adult wages, he goes and marries. And if you would now go to Per Bakken, the crofter over the road (he holds the place from us), just for fun you could look into his corn bin to see if his wife has anything to cook for herself and the two young ones. It won't be much.'

I have heard many such points of view and have been given many such examples. But often I have thought to myself: 'How, I wonder, would the matter look if, instead of having merely individual cases before us, we could see the thing as a whole.'

There are so many circumstances that imperceptibly can affect our observations and judgements that one can find bias and extreme exaggeration on the part of even the most upright of men. It is important, therefore, to collect as much detailed evidence as possible so as to arrive at a sound judgement of a problem that is the subject of so many people's thoughts and conversations.

125 Up to now in this book, the returns made annually by the priests which we have used have contained nothing as to the social position of the people getting married. But on 25 April 1853, I wrote to all the priests in the Christiania and Christiansand Dioceses (except for the

priests in the Christiania Diocesan Deanery, i.e. Christiania Town and Akers Parish),[2] requesting that they would send me details from their parish registers relating to married people and to the parents of illegitimate children, in such a way that they took cognizance of a person's social class. I ventured to apply with this request to 197 priests and I had the satisfaction of getting the desired information from 158 of them. This information is a trust reposed in me. I stand in debt to them, a debt which I must repay by carefully working through the data and then publishing them, so that the men who have kindly assisted me in my enquiries are able to see the complete picture. That part of the data which concerns illegitimate children I must reserve for another essay. Here I shall present what I got regarding marriage in the different ranks of society.

126 Naturally one can talk about many ranks or classes of society, but in order to avoid too great a difficulty I have in these enquiries kept to a twofold division which I will call the propertied class (Class 1) and the working class (Class 2). And in order to show what I mean by these two classes, which are naturally only divided in an approximate, common-sense sort of way, I give here the schema which I set out in the letter to the priests and according to which, therefore, the facts for each parish are arranged.

'To Class 1 are reckoned (see the census tables for 1845, p. 26): public officials, public employees, university students, office workers, farmers (freeholders and lease holders), businessmen, factory owners, manufacturers, handworkers with a licence or actual handicraft masters, masters of vessels, and whichever other group is in a social position that is understood to stand nearest to those enumerated here.'

'To Class 2 are reckoned: crofters with or without land, men who clear land for wages, handworkers without a licence, sailors, ship's pilots, day-labourers, servants, and whichever other group is in a social position that is understood to stand nearest to those enumerated here.'

'To each class are also added related persons – widows, wives, children and other family members – in so far as they might not, by having a definite independent profession, be considered to belong to another class than that of the family head. So, for example, married people,

---

[2] I had presented the questions I wanted answered in a questionnaire with, altogether, 109 headings. To fill out these would, for such populous parishes as those in Christiania and Aker, demand a greater amount of work than I found I could reasonably request. I thought too that, perhaps, on some occasion I would find the time myself to consult the registers in these parishes, in order to collect the material for a special study of population conditions in the capital and its immediate neighbourhood; a study which, for various reasons, is desirable.

who were servants at the time they were married, or when their association was sealed, ought to be reckoned in Class 2, even if their parents pertain to Class 1.'

'When someone holds several positions, he ought to be allocated to the class to which he may be considered to belong by the position which, in economic respects, is the most important for him.'

'When one speaks, for example, of married couples of Class 1, one means by that couples of which the man belongs to the named class.'

It will be seen immediately that this is only an approximate classification. Another person would perhaps have done it differently. It goes without saying that not all the people of Class 1 are people with property or in a high position and that not all the people of Class 2 are merely working people or without resources. So, for example, it could happen that a farmer, and therefore a member of Class 1, is a very impoverished man, whilst on the other hand a crofter or factory worker could be in quite a good situation. But taken on the whole, everybody will find that those people who, according to my classification, are assigned to Class 1 by education or property or position of trust, stand above those who are assigned to Class 2. Or that, in general, it is the so-called upper classes which, by this classification, are set on the one side, and the so-called lower classes who are set over against them on the other.

127 Before I can turn to the matter itself may I quickly explain how I have made use of the mass of information. The data consisted of absolute totals and covered the two years 1851 and 1852. First of all I put together the totals for all the parishes belonging to the same deanery. Even so the data collected for a single deanery were not sufficient for statistical manipulation. I therefore continued summing the data, so forming larger groups by joining together several neighbouring deaneries. In this way I divided the two dioceses into seven groups, each of which comprised certain deanery districts, namely:

A. *Christiania Diocese*

Group 1 : (i) Nedre, (ii) Mellem, (iii) Vestre and (iv) Øvre Borgessyssel together with (v) Nedre Romerike deaneries.

Group 2 : (i) Øvre Romerike, Soløer and Odalen, ii) Østerdalen, (iii) Hedemarken and (iv) Gudbrandsdalen deaneries.[3]

Group 3 : (i) Thoten and Valders, (ii) Hadeland, Ringerike and Hallingdal as well as (iii) Kongsberg deaneries.

[3] So far as the Gudbrandsdalen, Thoten and Valders deaneries are concerned, the older division is followed here, under which the parishes of Gausdal and Faaberg belonged to the first-named.

Group 4: (i) Drammen, (ii) Nordre and (iii) Søndre Jarlsberg, (iv) Laurvik, (v) Bamble and (vi) Nedre Thelemarken deaneries.

B. Christiansand Diocese

Group 5: (i) Øvre Thelemarken østfjeldske and (ii) vestfjeldske deaneries, (iii) Østre and (iv) Vestre Nedenaes as well as (v) Robygdelaget deaneries.

Group 6: (i) Mandal, (ii) Lister and (iii) Dalerne deaneries.

Group 7: (i) Jaederen, (ii) Stavanger, (iii) Ryfylke and (iv) Karsmund deaneries.

As will be seen from this list I lack data not only, as stated, for the Christiania Diocesan Deanery, but also for the Christiansand Diocesan Deanery. But otherwise I have information for the majority of the parishes in the remaining districts. As the few parishes for which, as noted above, I lack information lie fairly evenly spread, I dare to believe that the data as I have ordered them give a fairly accurate picture of actual conditions.[4]

128 What we should first of all seek to discover, with the help of this information, is how the marriages were shared between the two classes. In this respect we have evidence on 8,933 couples and, therefore, for the same number of men as women married in the years 1851 and 1852. We now ask: to what extent did they belong to Class 1 or to Class 2? I have reckoned the relationship in percentages for both dioceses under one, for each of the two dioceses and for each of the seven groups. The result appears in Table 26.

If we now cast a glance at the bottom line of the table, the one giving figures for the combined dioceses, we see immediately that far more of the married men and women belong to Class 2 than to Class 1. If we look further at the figures for each of the two dioceses we find the same thing, only that the working class has not quite such a massive preponderance in the Christiansand Diocese as it has in the Christiania Diocese. If, finally, we examine the relationship in the seven groups, it appears as a general rule that there are more married in the working class than in the propertied class, a rule from which only Group 6 forms an exception.

---

[4] Apart from the fact that no information was received from some parishes, I have also been compelled to omit some, when the answers disclosed a misunderstanding of the questions. What degree of completeness the facts used in the following tables represent is best seen by comparing the sum total of marriages in the years 1851 and 1852, in the two dioceses (excepting both diocesan deaneries) with the number I have used. The former figure was 11,310, the latter 8,933.

Table 26. *Number of brides and bridegrooms belonging to the propertied class (Class 1) and the working class (Class 2) as a percentage of all brides and bridegrooms in the dioceses of Christiania and Christiansand and their constituent parts, 1851 and 1852*

	Men		Women	
Place	Class 1	Class 2	Class 1	Class 2
Group 1	32	68	34	66
Group 2	34	66	34	66
Group 3	36	64	36	64
Group 4	35	65	33	67
Group 5	40	60	40	60
Group 6	63	37	60	40
Group 7	45	55	46	54
Christiania Diocese	34	66	34	66
Christiansand Diocese	48	52	47	53
Both dioceses	38	62	37	63

But the fact that nearly everywhere there are more working-class married couples than ones from the propertied class must not immediately be explained by saying that people in the former class are so very much quicker to marry than people in the latter. For this would be an overhasty and incorrect explanation. What, primarily, we learn from the table, is not the greater or lesser frequency of marriage amongst the two classes, but simply which of the two classes contains the greatest number of people and by about how much the total of the one class is greater than that of the other. For it is reasonable to suppose that in the class which has the greatest number of people there will occur, on average, the most marriages.

It is important, however, for the investigation that follows to know that, in most places, the working class is so very much more numerous than the propertied class. And it ought to be noted that, whilst this difference in the Christiania Diocese is very great, it is smaller in the Christiansand Diocese. Indeed in that diocese one group (Group 6) forms such an exception that the opposite situation occurs, that is, there are more people of the propertied than of the working class. Most simply and intelligibly we could put the matter thus: in the eastern districts the population consists of fewer masters and more servants and workmen employed by them. In the western districts wealth is more evenly distributed, so that the propertied class neither have need of, nor could they provide employment for, so many working people.

129 The difference in the size of the two classes that we find in this country must, it is evident, have a great influence in many directions. A group of people can make a State, so we can talk about the political constitution of the society and its influence upon the welfare of its citizens. But a people can also be looked upon as a great family, whose many members are kept together by the many invisible ties between neighbours and acquaintances, masters and servants, public officials and ordinary citizens, high and low. Regarding this we talk about the social structure of society. The political constitution of a State can be changed in a day. Social arrangements, the traditional ordering of society between the different classes, cannot be changed so easily or so fast. The social life of a people is like the soil in which one skilfully plants the tree of the political order, sometimes with and sometimes without luck. It is because of this that it is worthwhile paying attention to each and every feature which in any way contributes to informing us of the relationship between the different classes in society.

One such feature I shall present here. It occurred to me to ask: how often does it happen that marriages take place between the higher and lower classes? How often for instance does it occur that the son of a crofter gets to marry the daughter of a farmer or that the son of a farmer marries the daughter of a crofter? Or to what extent do people in our country marry within their own social class? I have got an answer to this question with regard to each of the previously mentioned 8,933 couples. The result appears in Table 27.

Table 27. *Intra- and inter-class marriages in the dioceses of Christiania and Christiansand and their constituent parts, 1851 and 1852*

Place	From 100 men of Class 1 there were married with women of:		From 100 men of Class 2 there were married with women of:	
	Class 1	Class 2	Class 1	Class 2
Group 1	78	22	12	88
Group 2	79	21	11	89
Group 3	86	14	8	92
Group 4	78	22	8	92
Group 5	74	26	17	83
Group 6	75	25	34	66
Group 7	77	23	20	80
Christiania Diocese	80	20	10	90
Christiansand Diocese	76	24	22	78
Both dioceses	79	21	12	88

130 When looking at this table too we begin at the bottom line. It shows us that in the two dioceses combined the situation was as follows. Of 100 men in the propertied class, 79 married within their own class whilst the remaining 21 married women of the working class. Furthermore, of 100 men of the working class, 88 married within their own class and only 12 took wives from the propertied class.

That is what it looks like if we use percentages. If, however, we look at the absolute totals on which this calculation is based, we find the remarkable fact that in reality the situation in the two classes is the same. For 716 women belonging to Class 2, by marrying men of the propertied class, were raised up into Class 1, whilst, on the other hand, 681 women of Class 1 went down to Class 2. There is, as there necessarily has to be, a certain balance here.

But I turn back to the table and notice there is some difference between the two dioceses. Intermarriage happens less frequently in the Christiania Diocese than in the Christiansand Diocese. Indeed, we find this difference if we compare any of the four eastern districts with any of the three western ones. We see that, in particular, in Group 6, men of the working class quite often marry women from the propertied class.

But there was also a corresponding difference in the relative size of the two classes in the two dioceses. If we now take Tables 26 and 27 together, we find that in the Christiania Diocese, where the working class is the more numerous, intermarriage is less frequent than it is in the Christiansand Diocese (especially in Group 6) where the working class is less numerous.

We come to the conclusion that where there is a great difference in size between the propertied and the working class (few people of property as against many working people) there is also a great difference in habits and ways of thought. The former are seen as separated from the latter, and at any rate do not marry readily outside their own class. Where, on the other hand, the difference in the membership of the two classes is smaller, then the gap between them is smaller so that one feels itself more the equal of the other.

Now many will probably say immediately that the more equality and feeling of equality between man and man, the better. Indeed the less difference there is between the propertied and the working class, both in numbers and in living conditions and customs, the happier it is for both parties. This would, though, be too quick a judgement. No doubt it is not difficult to prove what crises and difficulties can develop in a society that has a numerous working population and a small group of managerial and propertied people who keep themselves aloof from the former less-favoured class. But it is almost as easy to show how unfortunate it can be for the development of the economy and the advancement of education and culture when property is in many hands, so that one gets no diversity in the life of society. It is, however, reasonable to continue enquiries in this direction, to make comparisons between the different parts of the kingdom. For this should lead to interesting findings and explanations of the customs of the people and their wellbeing. One such line of enquiry should be precisely these interclass marriages.

131 The majority of people marry only once. That one who has become a widower or a widow marries a second time is indeed rarer. But in this matter too there does appear a certain regularity. Earlier (p. 118) I said that in certain districts it happens year after year, quite regularly, that several widowers and widows remarry. I pointed out how this was based in a variety of ways upon the customs and circumstances of the people. Now one asks: do there appear to be any constant differences in this matter between the two classes, bearing in mind that their circumstances and conditions are in many ways so very different? The data from 1851 and 1852 contain the answer to this. It is presented in Table 28.

Table 28. *Civil status of men and women of the propertied class (Class 1) and the working class (Class 2) at marriage in the dioceses of Christiania and Christiansand, 1851 and 1852*

Place	Bachelor and spinster	Bachelor and widow	Widower and spinster	Widower and widow
Class 1				
Christiania Diocese	83	5	10	2
Christiansand Diocese	82	4	12	2
Both dioceses	83	5	10	2
Class 2				
Christiania Diocese	88	3	7	2
Christiansand Diocese	85	4	8	3
Both dioceses	88	3	7	2

Here we really do find a difference between the two classes. For in Class 1 there are more, but in Class 2 fewer widowers or widows, amongst the marrying couples – at any rate in the Christiania Diocese.

This difference is reasonable enough. If it is so, as I suggested earlier (para. 111), that bachelors sometimes marry widows as a calculated act (e.g. 'to get a plot of land') it is to be expected that such a thing would more often occur amongst rich people, where plots of land and other such wonderful things are to be found. If a widower of the working class, poor man, should think about getting married again he is more likely to hesitate, given that he must first share his poor home with his children, for he will have little or nothing left for his new household.

132 From Table 28 we can see the proof of what has just been said, namely that the majority of married couples are the product of marriages between bachelors and spinsters. These couples are usually the youngest (for it is the somewhat older bachelors who marry widows and the somewhat older spinsters who marry widowers).

And now we shall look in particular at the ages of the bachelors and spinsters who married each other and see what differences there might be between the two classes in this respect. In this essay, where we have the condition of reckless marriages continually before our eyes, this is a matter of the greatest importance. For a very young age of marriage would give the impression that it was reckless and premature.

So, how old were the bachelors and spinsters of the propertied and working class when they got married?[5] How many were there under 20 years of age, between 20 and 25 years etc.? The answer is to be found in Table 29, which again is based on the data from the years 1851 and 1852.

How often have I heard the assertion that boys of the working class marry so early that most of them are no more than 22 or 23 years of age! For that reason therefore this table is of the greatest interest to me. It shows that this assertion is as incorrect as it is damaging. Of 100 bridegrooms of Class 2 there were only about 28 or 29 between 20 and 25 years of age and of these again only a few must have been as young as 22 or 23 years. Those who would have it that the people of the working class marry early, that poor men's children are hardly confirmed or have barely stopped receiving parish relief before they start to think about such foolishness, that the son of the crofter has scarcely started to work and learn something before he goes to the minister and wants to get married etc. – that sort of talk ought to be done away with after this. It has nothing to do with reality. It is an unjustifiable exaggeration.

133 Generally speaking it is somewhat difficult to grasp all that the table contains. It is difficult to see and retain the many figures which are involved when comparing the different classes. Given the complexity of the data it will quickly become impossible to get a view of the situation in the different districts of the seven groups.

---

[5] Whether a married couple (the marriage being of a bachelor and a spinster) is here reckoned in Class 1 or Class 2, depends upon whether the husband belonged to Class 1 or Class 2, no regard being paid to the wife's previous position or class.

Table 29. *Age at marriage of bachelors and spinsters of the propertied class (Class 1) and the working class (Class 2) in the dioceses of Christiania and Christiansand, 1851 and 1852*

Years	Christiania Diocese				Christiansand Diocese				Both dioceses			
	Class 1		Class 2		Class 1		Class 2		Class 1		Class 2	
	B.	S.	B.	S.	B.	S.	B.	S.	B.	S.	B.	S.
	%	%	%	%	%	%	%	%	%	%	%	%
Under 20	0.5	7.2	0.7	3.5	1.0	10.8	0.7	5.2	0.7	8.4	0.7	3.9
20–25	23.4	42.2	29.2	38.5	21.6	44.3	26.6	40.5	22.8	42.9	28.7	38.9
25–30	39.8	34.4	45.0	39.8	39.2	31.8	46.3	37.1	39.6	33.6	45.3	39.2
30–40	31.0	14.9	22.7	16.6	33.0	11.9	23.2	14.8	31.7	13.9	22.8	16.2
40–50	4.3	1.1	2.1	1.5	4.4	1.2	2.7	2.1	4.3	1.1	2.2	1.6
Over 50	1.0	0.2	0.3	0.1	0.8	0.0	0.5	0.3	0.9	0.1	0.3	0.2
Total	100	100	100	100	100	100	100	100	100	100	100	100

B. = Bachelor   S. = Spinster

I can, however, present the whole in another, simpler way. I know, for instance, how many old and young bridegrooms there were in each class and if I put together the youngest and oldest ages, adding something to the first, subtracting something from the second (all according to certain rules of mathematics) I can find out how old the bridegrooms were on average, or – as I could have expressed it – how old the average bridegroom was.[6] I give these average ages in Table 30.

Table 30. *Mean age at marriage of bridegrooms and brides of the propertied class (Class 1) and the working class (Class 2) in the dioceses of Christiania and Christiansand, 1851 and 1852*

	Bridegroom		Bride	
Place	Class 1	Class 2	Class 1	Class 2
	years	years	years	years
Group 1	30.1	28.3	26.4	26.9
Group 2	30.0	28.2	26.5	27.1
Group 3	29.0	27.7	25.9	26.4
Group 4	29.2	28.2	25.8	26.7
Group 5	29.9	28.6	25.4	26.2
Group 6	29.9	28.7	25.9	27.0
Group 7	29.5	28.1	25.0	26.9
Christiania Diocese	29.6	28.1	26.2	26.8
Christiansand Diocese	29.8	28.4	25.5	26.6
Both dioceses	29.7	28.2	25.9	26.8

134 The average age of a bridegroom in Class 1 is, according to Table 30, in both dioceses combined, close to 30 years. When we look

[6] The procedure is this. Instead of, as in Table 29, giving the ages in the form of 'under 20 years', 'between 20 and 25 years', and so on, I imagine these ages as being – 19, $22\frac{1}{2}$, $27\frac{1}{2}$, 35, 45, and $52\frac{1}{2}$. I then calculate how long the people have lived and divide this figure equally between them. By way of example I give the calculation so far as the bridegrooms of Class 1 are concerned, for the Christiania Diocese:

Age	Number of bridegrooms	The sum of the ages of all bridegrooms
19 years	9	171
$22\frac{1}{2}$	414	9,315
$27\frac{1}{2}$	706	19,415
35	550	19,250
45	76	3,420
$52\frac{1}{2}$	17	892
All ages	1,772	52,463

When 1,772 bridegrooms have lived a total number of 52,463 years, then the average age is to be found by dividing the second total by the first, which gives $29\frac{6}{10}$ years.

at the situation in the individual districts or groups, we find that in no place is it under 29 years, whilst in only one place is it a little over 30 years. The average age of a bridegroom in Class 2, on the other hand, in both dioceses combined, is only a little over 28 years. In none of the groups does it reach up to 29 years, which was the lowest limit for the average age in Class 1. In that respect the general opinion is quite correct: men from the working class marry earlier than men from the propertied class, though the difference is not so great as most people may have thought. On the other hand this contention is not correct when it refers to working-class people as a whole. For if we investigate the conditions relative to the women, the table shows the opposite to be the case. In both dioceses together and separately, as well as in each of the seven groups, the average age of the brides in Class 1 is lower than in Class 2.

I show this most important fact more clearly in Table 31.

Table 31. *Differences between the mean ages of bridegrooms and of brides in the propertied class (Class 1) and the working class (Class 2) in the dioceses of Christiania and Christiansand, 1851 and 1852*

Place	By how much the bridegrooms of Class 1 are *older* than those of Class 2	By how much the brides of Class 1 are *younger* than those of Class 2
	years	years
Group 1	1.8	0.5
Group 2	1.8	0.6
Group 3	1.3	0.5
Group 4	1.1	0.9
Group 5	1.3	0.8
Group 6	1.2	1.1
Group 7	1.4	1.9
Christiania Diocese	1.5	0.6
Christiansand Diocese	1.4	1.1
Both dioceses	1.5	0.9

Even the most fleeting glance at this table shows us that the bridegrooms of Class 1 are everywhere older than those of Class 2, whereas the brides of Class 1 are everywhere younger than those of Class 2. We also find that the age difference is very similar overall, never under one or over two years on the part of the bridegrooms, never under one half and seldom over one year on the part of the brides. When we think what a difference there is between, for example the upland districts of the Christiania Diocese and the coastal districts of the Christiansand Diocese – differences in the economy, in the number of people in the

upper and lower classes, in the social interaction between the classes –
it really is quite remarkable that in this matter there should be so much
similarity overall and that the age differences are as uniform as they
appear to be.

135 I must draw attention to something which the last but one table
taught us. Both in Class 1 and in Class 2 we see that in general the
bridegrooms are older than the brides. But this age gap is not the same
in both classes. In Class 1 the age difference between bride and bridegroom is greater than in Class 2. The situation will be seen more clearly
in Table 32.

Table 32. *Mean number of years by which bridegrooms were older
than their brides in the propertied class (Class 1) and the
working class (Class 2) in the dioceses of Christiania and
Christiansand, 1851 and 1852*

Place	In Class 1	In Class 2
	years	years
Group 1	3.7	1.4
Group 2	3.5	1.1
Group 3	3.1	1.3
Group 4	3.5	1.5
Group 5	4.5	2.4
Group 6	4.0	1.7
Group 7	4.5	1.2
Christiania Diocese	3.4	1.3
Christiansand Diocese	4.3	1.8
Both dioceses	3.8	1.4

In Class 1 we see that the average age of the bridegroom is between
3 and 4½ years greater than that of the bride. In Class 2, on the other
hand, this age difference is only between 1 and 2 years.[7]

136 Putting together the information contained in Tables 31 and 32

---

[7] In this matter of the age difference between the bride and bridegroom, it must
be remembered that it is the average age which we have here before us. In actual
fact the majority of bridegrooms take younger brides, some take brides of the
same age as themselves, and some brides who are older than they are. But we are
concerned with the matter as a whole, and if we use the average age as the basis
for comparison, we find that the age of the bridegrooms was greater than the
age of the brides in both classes. But in Class 2 this age difference is not so great
as in Class 1. This must be due to the fact that in Class 2 not so many bridegrooms were marrying younger brides, more, on the other hand, taking ones of
their own age or older. More precise comparisons could be made, had we the
data showing us for example how many of the brides were more than 10 years
younger, and how many more than 10 years older than their bridegrooms, in
each of the two classes.

it would appear that bachelors of the propertied class marry somewhat later than do the bachelors of the working class. The former, however, chose younger brides than do the latter. Thus the age difference between bride and bridegroom is greater in the propertied class than it is in the working class. This is the situation we found in both the Christiania and the Christiansand Dioceses in the years 1851 and 1852. We do not know if the situation was the same in earlier periods or if it is the same in other dioceses and in other countries. But when the matter is shown to be so extraordinarily similar in each of the two dioceses, indeed even in each of the seven smaller districts into which we have divided the dioceses, then we know for certain that it is not some chance occurrence that has produced it, rather that there must be certain definite, general reasons, the effects of which we have before us.

137 It is indeed natural that the average age of the bridegroom is greater than that of the bride. It goes together with facts of nature, that, in comparison with girls, boys develop for the most part more slowly, with regard to both body and mind and are, therefore, fully grown at a later age. It is here as with certain types of trees that some are later than others in putting forth their leaves and flowers in the spring. But besides these natural circumstances, which are probably the same in both classes, there must be certain features within those social conditions that determine the internal and external characteristics of the upper and lower classes, which cause the age gap between bride and bridegroom to be different in the two classes.

The needle of a magnet seldom, or never, points due north, but usually deviates, in some places towards the west, in others towards the east. This is something which naturalists from endless observations and enquiries have striven to fathom. Now my tables also deviate towards the west and towards the east. In one circle of society I see one rule guiding the behaviour and practice of the people, whilst in another circle I find a different one. What is the true north here, about which the variations turn, and where are the magnetic poles that cause these mysterious deviations?

There is a certain natural difference in the ages at which young men and young women mature and we can imagine that if people lived in such a happy natural state that, willingly and without hindrance, they followed the signs of nature, then the age difference between bridegroom and bride would always be the same. What has happened in actual life, in our somewhat contrived social life? One wonders if, owing to certain circumstances, the age difference has become greater in the upper classes, or if, owing to certain contrary circumstances, it has decreased in the working class? What has happened?[8]

Naturally I know that for a complete analysis of this matter a greater series of observations would be required than it has so far been possible to make. One can say that the question concerns the primary and essential differences in the circumstances and practices of the upper and lower classes of the population. For marriage is an affair of the human heart and all the circumstances of one's life, the outer as well as the inner, consciously or unconsciously influence one's relationship to it. In the meantime because the matter is so wide-ranging and so important it is worthwhile seeing how far one can come in solving the riddle. What may be dim and unsure today, another day may teach us.

138 Why, in particular, young men of the propertied class put off marriage somewhat longer than do boys of the working class, does not seem so difficult to understand. The man who is born and brought up in better circumstances comes involuntarily to consider it his duty to work himself forward to a position at least as good as and as independent as his father's. But this usually requires both time and application. The son of the ship's captain goes to sea beginning his trade as an ordinary seaman and subsequently becoming an able seaman. But given the ideas and aspirations he has taken with him from home, he probably cannot leave it at that. He holds out patiently until he becomes a mate and finally gets a ship to command. Now perhaps just at the same time as he gets his master's ticket, a sailor who is the same age as he comes to him with his twelve-year-old son asking that the new skipper should take the lad along as a cabin-boy. Yet the skipper himself has not even dared to think about establishing a family. Of the doubtless few boys who marry under the age of 20 I dare say the majority are the sons of farmers who, owing to their father's death, must take over the farm. More usually, the eldest son of the farmer must wait quite a long time however before he can step into his father's farm. The younger sons are usually so affected by the thinking of their class that they do not seem to conceive any other means of livelihood than having a farm to run. For this reason they also must wait a long time before they dare come to a decision about getting married. The crofter's son, on the other hand, or the servant-boy, who sees his livelihood more in his health and

[8] In the Norwegian Law of 1687, 3–18–5, where it is said that people under age must not be betrothed, the coming-of-age for a boy is set at his 20th birthday, and for a girl at her 16th. So the difference in age was four years. This age difference is very close to that which we have found between bridegroom and bride in Class 1 (3.8 years).

his strong arms, can at 25 years of age believe he has what he needs and finds that he might just as well marry early as late. The university graduate thinks perhaps of becoming a professor, so he must expend as little time as possible on earning money and as many hours as possible, by day and by night, in adding to his store of knowledge. But this is not understood by the quarryman who from home has been used to nothing but living from hand to mouth, as it is called, whilst his art is already learnt to perfection at an early age. Now if he, instead of marrying at the age of 25, would delay until he becomes 27, he would in that space of time be able to save a shilling or two, which would be useful enough. But perhaps it is just as well that he marries young. If he is honest and talented enough to win a fine wife and prepare for himself and for her a happy domestic life then he will in a happy way be preserved from the temptations which, in a long bachelor life, may possibly become too dangerous for him. For quarrymen and such coarse workmen have so little skill in arranging matters pleasantly in their lodgings where they spend their rest time and their holidays, that the seduction of evil society easily gets its grip on them.

139 'Tell me', I asked a crofter with whom I sat out on the hillside and talked about many things, 'Tell me, Ole, you married when you were 23 years old. Don't you think now when you think back over the matter that it was folly to marry so early?'

'No, I cannot say that.'

'Is that so! I must confess that I am very pleased with what I have seen and heard in your house. You have six handsome, well-fed children who are indeed so cheerful and lively in your living-room that we have been compelled to come out here just to get sufficient peace and quiet to talk together. You don't suffer from want now and you have certainly never taken help from any man. You seem to be a good work-man and your wife is certainly very clever in running both the house and the children. But I still say that you were not really grown up when, at 23, you went to the minister and asked for the banns to be published. You were a boy who could not have really thought about what he took upon himself – don't you agree?'

'I thought it was the best what I did. For when one marries so early one has youth on one's side, to work for the young ones and to get them out into the world before old age comes.'

'Nonsense, you didn't think in that way about it.'

'Yes, I did.'

'And you will have me believe that?'

'Yes, it really is true. I remember it well. One often sees people falling into complete poverty when they are old and still have small children. For you can still have many children even if you marry very late. That was the case with my parents. I was the eldest and out in service, but at home there were many small children. Earnings were small and things were bad.'

And in this way Ole actually got me to believe his explanation, especially as it was by no means a new one. I have often found instances of the same way of thinking amongst the working class. What shall one call such thoughtfulness in the young? It is exactly the reverse of recklessness and one feels uncomfortable to see youth's shining hope change into the anxieties of old age. But it is fairly certain that such motives hardly apply in the higher, educated and wealthy classes. We may, therefore, in this instance, see one of the reasons for the different ages of marriage of the men in the two classes.

140 I was really very charmed by a young, cheerful postillion who sat at the back of my carriage, and I entertained myself by listening to how the world went with him. He was a servant and had fairly recently got full wages. He had saved a half-score *dollars* from his earlier poor wages. It seemed to me a good sign.

'Now you are 20 years old my boy. When in eight years time I come travelling this way again I would be pleased to visit you on an excellent croft. By then you will probably have found someone who can help you to keep house.'

'I am married', he said.

'No, listen to me seriously', I continued, 'I dare say it wouldn't be difficult for you to find a sweetheart, but it is not so easy to get a decent place at the present time, it will come then if – .'

'Yes, but I am married already', continued the boy with such fervour that I had to turn round and look at him.

'You are married? At your age? Didn't you say you were 20 years old?'

'Yes, I was 20 in the spring and it was then I had my wedding.' I laughed and ticked him off.

'Yes, my master told me off as well. For when he knew that my girl was with child, he wanted me to travel away to Nordland. For there were many boys who did so, and there was such a lack of places in the parish that there would be nothing but mischief if the girl and I married. But that made me so angry that on the same day I went to the priest and asked for the banns to be published. The day we were married our child was baptized. I thought that once it had come to this I ought to take matters seriously. And since then I have both sweetheart and

child at my parents. Yet it hasn't cost them anything, for we have man-
aged ourselves up to now.'

Often since, I have thought about this resolute young man, hoping
with the best will in the world that his cheerful spirit would not be too
bitterly disappointed. I have often been forced to remember him, for
I have often met the same situation, and so have noticed a new reason
for early marriage in the working class – early but not necessarily reckless. The manner in which young people make each other's acquaintance – the nightly visit upheld by the old customs and domestic circumstances of the countryside – is attended by much thoughtlessness. But
when the girl must tell the boy that she is with child, it can very well
be that he goes with heavy steps to the minister and asks for the banns
to be published and the wedding solemnized. So by one reckless marriage, as perhaps he hears people say, he may fulfil his important duties
to the child and its mother and, in a way, make good what wrong he
has done. But this occurs more frequently in the working class than in
the propertied class for two reasons. First, the moral situation is better
in the propertied class, in so far as it is less common for its sons to do
wrong in this way. Secondly, the better-off man's son who actually lets
himself be carried away, for the most part does wrong with a servant-
girl, or another woman of the poorer classes. He then finds it unreasonable that he should stand by his promises and by marrying the girl give
her back the honour of which, perhaps, his false promises have robbed
her. Whilst the poor boy thinks there is no other way than that he must
marry the girl, the wealthy boy sends away the girl he has seduced with
a few *shillings* to help bring up the child. He puts off marriage until,
perhaps later, he finds the opportunity to make a fortunate match with
a person of his own rank, a match which, more often than many would
think, is made bitter by the recollection of that false step of youth.[9]

141 So a series of observations and experiences help us, in some
measure to explain the first part of the somewhat involved conditions
drawn to our attention by Tables 30, 31 and 32, namely that bachelors
of the propertied class are, in general, older on their wedding day than
bachelors of the working class. But why is it that the girls whom the
latter chose as wives are usually older than the wives of the former?
Why is it that, in general, the bridegroom in the upper ranks of society

---

[9] The data, which I've already mentioned I got from the priests, show me that
though immorality of this kind is probably less frequent amongst the propertied
class, men of that class mostly find their victims amongst girls of the lower
classes, seldom marrying the mothers of their illegitimate children. But the details
of these enquiries I must keep for another essay.

is about 4 years older, but in the lower ranks, on the other hand, only about $1\frac{1}{2}$ years older than his bride? For that was the other matter which we found in those same tables.

A closer investigation brings us to the question of the position of women in the different circles of society.

Amongst barbaric tribes we see the woman as man's degraded slave. Where civilization is at its most advanced, in what we might call over-refined circles, she is paid homage as a mistress. These are the extremes. Usually we could say that our entire culture, prevailing manners and ideas, everything that has meaning in human life, is instrumental in determining the woman's worth in a man's and in her own eyes, as well as her rights and duties in domestic and civil society, her circumstances and position in life. And above all the introduction of Christianity in human life shows itself as a turning point in the history of women. It is one of Christianity's great benefactions to mankind that women have come into their own as man's joint heir to life and as a worthy object for his loving regard. And if all is well in this matter, there is peace and happiness in the homes of our country. The growing generation is brought up with good manners. If there is vigour and life in the soul of the people, then this is due, not least, to the influence of Christianity.

But it may well be that a closer consideration of this matter, as of several others, will show us how from olden times – from heathenism – views and opinions have been handed down. These existed for a long time and in parts still do exist by the side of the imported and the foreign. In olden times it was the case that a man bought his wife. It was expressly called 'buying', since it was the girl's father or brother or nearest male relative who had to arrange for her marriage and had to determine how much she should get as dowry and how great a sum in money and goods must be given by him who would have the girl. That dowry and this settlement was considered to be the property of the wife, her share of the estate. With this property she had a certain independence of position as against her husband. If they lived well together then they could consider the property as common and could add it to the common pool. If the position was less happy, and the wife was threatened with injury by a coarse husband, then she could see herself divorced from him, take her property with her and live by herself. That 'buying' was, therefore, what we would now call a contract. Marriage was more a domestic union than a pact of the heart. Then came Christianity and little by little laws and regulations were laid down to enforce the rule that what God had joined together man should not set apart. The marriage pact was therefore more heartfelt and more permanent.

But as recently as under the government of Christian IV, we can still see, in the provisions of the country's laws, that the girl's father and mother or, if they are not alive, her next paternal relatives, should arrange for her marriage and make an agreement about the size of her dowry and settlement. (If the girl married without their advice she forfeited her inheritance.) When the girl has become a wife, she should still keep a separate account of her property so that her husband would not be able to squander it.[10] Not quite so many directions as regards marriage are given in the Law of 1687. Furthermore it is said here that it is not only the parents who should rule the girl since her consent shall mean something also. Nevertheless the law still pays great regard to the economic side of the matter and therefore assigns the guardian great power, as he can control the girl's property if she marries without his consent. In particular, regulations were made providing for the situation where the guardian, for the sake of his own profit, misuses his power and refuses to let the girl marry, even if she could make a good match.[11]

142 Such was how the law defined the matter. Such, naturally, was also the custom and opinion of the country. But this way of thinking has continued until today amongst a very numerous section of the Norwegian people, especially amongst a great part of the farming class in the somewhat remote districts. Agreements about marriage are probably no longer called a business and it is no doubt unusual for formal agreements to be made about the dowry and settlement between the girl's father and the suitor.[12] Nevertheless both sides think about the wealth each of the parties brings with them and these considerations often have a great deal of influence upon the decisions. It is often said that the majority of marriages established amongst the farming class are pure marriages of convenience. I would not go as far as that. Marriages can often be considered only as profitable contracts, domestic agreements by which the man and woman will be better off in a material sense than if they lived separately. Here no doubt there is less thought about marriage's great meaning for people's inner life and about the feelings of affection, devotion and love that must not be absent in a marriage that is to be truly happy. But such are the views and opinions that have been inherited from earlier times. On the whole

[10] Christian IV's Norwegian Law Book of 1604, *Inheritance*, Chs. 1, 2 and 3.
[11] Norwegian Laws, Bk 3, Ch. 18.
[12] Although I know a parish (Lom in Gudbrandsdalen) where, now and then, agreements are still made (or at least were up to fairly recently) as to what sum of money should be paid by whichever of the parties breaks off an engagement – should that happen.

the Norwegian farmer's life is characterized by a marked tranquillity and sound good sense and to this could well be united the virtues of fidelity which, to such a high degree and with such very few exceptions, adorn married life in our country districts. So now, when some young people, brought up to this way of thinking, attend essentially to the material benefits and profits of the marriage pact, I am of the opinion that one should not be so quick to reproach them with the fact that they have consciously and upon reflection repressed the voice of the heart, which is what townspeople condemn as marriages of convenience. Rather should one feel sorry for those whose inner lives are still so little developed that they have not properly been able to apprehend and enjoy that which should be the best and most beautiful thing in marriage, the mutual tender love of a man and a woman.

All this must ensure that amongst the farming class the bridegroom is usually older than his bride. Here I should make clear that by the farming class (which make up the greatest part of what I have called Class 1, and which has held to the views and opinions of earlier times), I mean the farmers and not their labourers and crofters. For when we look away from the exceptions, a large number of which always occur, we are able to present the matter as follows. The son of a farmer always goes about with the thought of a good match and with great diligence seeks to find and win a girl whose inheritance or dowry can help him pay for a farm. As soon as a wealthy man's daughter has grown up she becomes a good match and she is soon certain to see many suitors. But since the good matches are always few as against the many who seek them, the majority of the latter must see their hopes disappointed for many years. Often then it is an elderly bachelor and a fairly young girl who in the end are united.

143 Up until now I have presented the position as to marriage amongst the farmer class as something which, on the whole, can be regarded as irreproachable and in certain respects even laudable. But it is indeed very reasonable to assume that the intellect can so take the upper hand that one gets heartlessness and baseness. An example will make this clear. The eldest son of one of the most esteemed farming families (on account of their wealth) in a certain old-fashioned parish was engaged to a fine girl of an equally good family from one of the neighbouring farms. He had probably not made an agreement with her parents (for this is often put off until one fixes the wedding day and makes all the necessary arrangements for bringing about the marriage) but he was engaged to the girl in the manner prevailing in the countryside, namely that he had won her consent and her parent's goodwill. So

he could, for example, come to the farm on Saturday evenings, share supper with the people of the house, sleep in the girl's arms and so in the morning be treated to coffee etc. This intimate relationship had been going on for some time and according to the custom of the parish there was nothing wrong with it. But then the boy stopped making his accustomed visits and the reason was that in another part of the district there lived a farmer whose farm was notable for having two mountain pastures (*saeters*). For the most part the farmer himself used only one of these and the other lay in such a position that it would be particularly convenient for the farm which the boy was to inherit and which had always lacked at good *saeter*. The same farmer had a daughter, fairly recently confirmed. What now? For one reason or another the boy believed that he would not be considered an unworthy suitor, for such matters are usually the subject of minute attention not only amongst the youth of the district but also amongst the older people. And there are usually one or two people who, for different reasons, have an interest in going between the parties making suggestions and giving advice. Furthermore, he himself actually put his case formally to the girl's father, taking an older relative with him as a precautionary measure. His offer could not be rejected out of hand. The boy was long past his reckless years, of good family and would inherit a fine farm from his father which, as far as one knew, was not encumbered with debt. Negotiations were therefore opened. Only the father showed a degree of caution in that he repeatedly prevented the boy from visiting the girl at night, something he was able to do without giving offence, because in the neighbourhood there lived one of the boy's relatives with whom he could take a night's lodging. But what happened? The father discovered from his enquiries that the boy had been engaged to another girl who now found herself in a highly pregnant condition. Suddenly all the negotiations were broken off. The story, which was generally well known in the district, was told to me by the father of the girl who was so happily saved from the shabby boy's greed. The story is therefore true, and with this and many other examples before our eyes I hazard the opinion that people who are acquainted with rural conditions will grant that I was correct when I say that although it is to be hoped that only a few farmers' sons show such a degree of baseness as the example I have just given revealed, it happens not so seldom that young men of the farmer class repress the voice of the heart and court and marry purely for the sake of the dowry. It has happened, not once but many times, that a boy who perhaps at 27 years of age was in a position to establish a family, has nevertheless waited until he becomes

37 and then for the heartless reason that by that time a certain rich farmer's daughter will have grown up to a marriageable age and by then he will be able to win her father's consent to carry home to his house both the girl and her fortune. Every time this happens, so increases the number of married couples in the propertied class where the man is much older than the bride.

144 What we have given up to now has concerned the farmer class, in which, as we have said, earlier opinions and thoughts have lasted longest. And the farmers form the most numerous part of what I have called the propertied class or Class 1. But if we look at the remaining members of this class – ships' captains, businessmen, handicraft masters, office holders, graduates etc., then a fairly clear explanation emerges of the condition we are dealing with, namely that the bridegroom is usually a good deal older than his bride. The higher education which these people on the whole possess has probably influenced their way of thinking in general, so that, in choosing their bride, they do not look so much at her prospective inheritance, nor, for the sake of material profit, aim to induce the fathers to give their youngish daughters into their power. Besides the way of thinking prevalent amongst the town population disapproves of such a thing. On the other hand, we must find it reasonable to suppose that the educated young man who by application has worked himself up to an independent position, so that a dowry of a couple of hundred *dollars* is not for him so important, pays more attention to personal charm and attractiveness when choosing his bride. And what he seeks he most often finds in a young girl who is just in her blooming years.

145 But all this is to a great extent otherwise in the working class or in Class 2. The tables showed us that here the age difference between bride and bridegroom is less than in Class 1. By looking closely we discover considerable singularities in the views and customs which would seem, fairly naturally, to entail that it must be so that the young man in the working class should usually choose his bride from amongst somewhat older women.

The daughter of a cultured family is already at 18 years of age considered to be fully grown. She possesses the developed understanding and cultured spirit with which she will adorn the house into which the well-to-do and affectionate husband carries her. The 18-year-old daughter of a prosperous farmer also appears as a grown girl in the eyes of all the boys in the parish, for her inheritance will not be greater than it is then and what she is bound to lack in domestic experiences will come with the years. But that is not so with the 18-year-old daughter of a crofter. She perhaps is newly come into service on a farm. Not only that, she is constantly hearing that like all crofters' children she is very backward in womanly pursuits (her mistress finds that even the everyday yarn the girl has spun is so uneven, and either too loose or too tight, that a deal must be made with the head dairywoman so that she can be released from there for a whole day to learn how to warp the loom). What is more, the 23-year-old-boy who works on a neighbouring farm does not invite her to accompany him to the dance in the crofter's living-room on a Sunday, since she is so young. However, it is not taken amiss if she comes uninvited to the party just to look at the jollification, and it is possible that he, for the sake of neighbourliness, dances a single dance with her. But she is not one of the girls he sets his cap at (to spend 12 *shillings* for coffee and honey-cake represents great attentiveness). She is not the one whom he takes great pains to accompany home at night – this night wandering which for so many is the beginning of familiarity and love, later developed by regular nightly visits (Saturday visits) during which the young people become 'acquainted' (acquainted is about the same as being secretly engaged). The 23-year-old boy who has adult pay and performs a grown man's work reckons himself fully grown; the 18-year-old girl, on the other hand, is for him still only an adolescent. And he is perhaps so well brought up that he knows that it is not right for a grown-up boy to approach a girl in that intimate way with night visits etc. For first of all she has not sufficient understanding to act on her own account, and her parents, being a long way away, are even less able to advise her. And secondly, honest fellow-servants and other people at the farm (for example, the trusted crofter who has the task of waking the girls in the morning) would fairly certainly reproach him if he 'slept' with the girl, who, since she is so young, it could not be his intention to marry. For it is something which has a firm hold here in this circle of society, that a good boy who thinks about marriage must seek a capable 'working person' and therefore stick to an older one who has got some knowledge and practice in womanly pursuits.

Such is a woman's position in this circle of society. The superior spirit and personal charm she might possess do not command a high price; dowry and inheritance there cannot be much to speak of. But the servant-boy has thoughts about the time when he will get a croft, and it is of the most obvious importance to him to get hold of a woman who can be a capable housewife and a cook and a milkmaid as well. If it happens that he must himself clear a holding, she must be able to help him move the logs which his axe has fashioned, while the food-sack hangs on the nearest branch of a pine and the child sleeps by its side. She must take a part in building the house and in collecting its contents.

146 A young boy who has not more than the few *dollars* he has saved from his servant's pay, marries a girl about his own age or a little older who has been so long in service and has used her pay so well that she, in addition to good wearing apparel and bed linen, owns a couple of pots, a baking pan, a couple of candlesticks and perhaps even a cow running with her master's herd. We see here a match of the type that is so very common amongst the working class in the countryside. Many perhaps will find it reasonable to suppose that he chooses her in particular because he knows that she has this small fortune, that he takes her for the sake of the pots and other valuables. But such an explanation is almost certainly incorrect. The servant-boy or crofter's son who knows that the work of himself and his wife must be their livelihood, is hardly tempted as much as the farmer's son to make his choice on such a basis. The farmer's son can hardly imagine any other way of earning a living than by getting the money to buy a farm. On the other hand, it is quite believable – and a good indication of the praiseworthy understanding in this class of society – that the boy sets great store by those useful things that have been collected, on the grounds that they are for him an infallible proof of the girl's thrift and shrewdness – housewifely qualities which he, as a result of his whole way of life, must necessarily rate very highly.

147 One ought not to imagine that in the exercise of his intelligence the young man necessarily smothered that liveliness of feeling and natural desire which ought to be present in the choice of a bride. But the calculus goes so far at times, and perhaps not so occasionally, that we fast lose sight of that optimistic view of life which should spur a youth on and guide his manhood. Once or twice I have, on a visit to a crofter's family, conceived a certain suspicion, and have then asked directly:

'Tell me, Nils, how was it possible that such an active boy as you could go out and take such an old one as a wife? She looks to me a capable person, but she is so much older than you.' The answer has sounded thus:

'I thought that when I took such an old woman the crowd of young ones would not be so great, for it is difficult for one who is in small circumstances to feed so many.'

Once there was a particularly unpleasant situation and when I had received the same answer almost in the same words, I replied, somewhat reluctantly:

'I think you have got a greater flock than any man should have.'

But unabashed the man continued:

'Yes, but the three young ones she had when we married don't hurt me at all, for the father of the one is a farmer and of the other two a tailor, who are in good positions, so there is no difficulty with the payments each year.'

Those who are so quick to censure the youth of the working class for their recklessness with regard to marriage, and their domestic affairs generally, might ponder what can well be the element in the position of the working class that calls for such an unnatural way of thinking and such a way of life.

148 That it so often happens in the working class that a younger boy marries an older girl can in many cases be caused by a particular initiative on the part of the girl. For it is possible that it is an older girl who courts a younger boy.

When the thing is put so straightforwardly it will seem highly offensive and unnatural to those of my readers who might not be aware of the particular rural conditions which I have in mind. But it is difficult to judge a single feature of lower-class life when one does not know the whole, and in order to be able to give a comprehensive explanation of this particular matter, I must enter into a little detail here.

On a dark and nasty autumn evening, a Saturday evening, Per, a young servant-boy, stands outside the kitchen window of a farm and stares in through the dark panes. The cold weather does not trouble him much for he is young, and besides he feels a strange new warmth in his breast each time the fire in the chimney flares up and he catches a glimpse of Anne, a fine servant-girl who sits by the spinning wheel between some other womenfolk. Patiently Per waits for an hour until Anne on some errand or other comes out of the farm house. Now he must take a grip on himself and with as little clumsiness as possible make use of this brief minute. So perhaps he himself does the errand and as he does so takes the opportunity to ask if she will be with him at the dance tomorrow. It is fairly certain that Anne understands what he is about and declines the invitation. But she is also inventive and knows how to give him such an acceptable reason that he cannot take her refusal ill and it is likely that he goes away with greater hope than when he came. The following Saturday he again gets into conversation with her and it is possible that he now notices more plainly that his visits are not disagreeable to her. It is fairly certain, therefore, that he is on the spot a third time and if she accepts a little cotton handkerchief he has got for her and, with a handshake, thanks him for it, he pays no heed to the snow and storm on the way home. The fourth Saturday evening he deliberately arranges matters so that he comes to the farm when the people there have gone to bed, and, almost as strongly as his heart beats in his breast, he beats on the window pane. He doesn't need to make much noise for, in all probability, Anne is expecting this to happen, and has lain awake until now. She comes out and at this late evening hour, when all other eyes are closed, she sits a long time and talks with him in the wood shed. They talk about whether or not there is a possibility at this time for people like them to get a holding or some other reasonable livelihood. The fifth evening he has more courage – 'Oh let me go in with you Anne' – and whilst a couple of girls and a boy snore around them in the room, the two sit on a bench and carry on a whispered conversation. The sixth evening – there must be no interruption in Per's Saturday visits as Anne might then think he is on the wing somewhere else – the sixth evening Anne is, by chance, very tired after one or two heavy jobs during the day. She lies down on the bed and allows him to sit on the edge of it. No doubt Anne is not alone in the bed. Little Mari lies together with her, but luckily Anne has her place on the outer edge. The seventh evening Per sits once again for a time on the edge of the bed, but then he kicks off his shoes and throws off his jacket and after a weak and short resistance on the part of Anne, lies by her side, flings his arms about her neck, repeats all his good promises, gets her consent and falls asleep. Anne takes care that he is on his feet and away again before any people of the house are up. But now Per and Anne are 'acquainted' (i.e. engaged) and these nightly visits will be repeated each Saturday. When they are secretly engaged, it is possible that on occasion another suitor slips in to Anne before Per. But I think Anne, as a fine girl, will know how to get him to the door ('No, we can't chat any more, I'm going to be up early tomorrow. I tell you Hans get on your way'). No doubt the situation cannot be kept secret very long, but it is a point of honour for fellow-servants not to disclose this kind of secret, and when it is found that they are true to each other so that she does not receive other boys, and he does not visit other girls, none of their acquaintances will blame or criticize them in the slightest. For this is the custom of the country in many of our rural districts and the only way by which young people of the servant class can become 'acquainted', and in many cases it is conducted in all modesty and faithfulness. This nightly courtship is naturally always extremely dangerous for flesh and blood. But it is a mistake to assume that all the girls who take to their lovers in this way are girls without modesty. In all classes where night courtship has its home there are rules for it which maintain a degree of strictness as to how modest girls must behave. Indeed, it is something which often occurs that a girl hands in her notice purely on the grounds that she cannot allow herself to be known to serve together with a girl who has gone against the prevailing rules and so got a bad reputation in the servant class.

But – to come back to the matter with which I began – as I have up to now depicted the situation between Per and Anne, it looks as if it was Per who took the first step. But it could very well have been Anne, and this same Anne can still be a modest girl both in her own estimation and in that of others. I myself believe Anne to be a steady and sensible girl, who has long recognized what life-long misfortune awaits a woman who embarks upon marriage with an unsteady boy. Anne has probably had offers from several such boys but prudently refused them all and thought that it would be best to work and collect some property for herself, so that she could at least live her life in her own way. But slowly the years go by. It happens that she begins to dread the thought of the burdens of a lifetime in service and the pain of a lonely old age, and probably by now she has turned the suitors away from her. But a capable working person, as she is, has something boyish or masculine in her nature, and it may well happen, that she, without being ashamed of herself, sets herself at some young and simple-hearted person like Per. An older boy, whom I dare say would rule both himself and her, pleases her not so much.

If she has, moreover, by long and faithful service won the esteem of her master, and with it the hope of getting a good croft from him if it should happen that she marries, then upon reflection she makes her decision and, with as much delicacy as is needed, she does small services for Per and shows him other acts of attention. This arouses tender thoughts on his part. With a girlish bashfulness he seeks her out that first Saturday evening, each time subsequently getting the new courage needed to effect a victory – a victory that was easier than he thought. But she will certainly stand by the honest boy whom she herself cares about.

And if we could visit them some years later, on their holding, we would certainly find that they live well together – although no doubt in a particular way. I picture him as a toiler who, after performing well his day's work, comes in tired and weary in the evening, eats his porridge and lies down to sleep, content now he has done what he should do. But it is his wife's views that prevail in the house. The difficulty of bringing up the children rests on her. It is her diligence and thrifty skill which keep the cow in such good condition on such poor fodder; that ensure the corn bin is never empty in spite of the poor harvest; that see there is always a little meat left in the house from last year's killing until the butchering season in the autumn; and that every second year provides Per with a fine new coat to go to church in, even though he has only two winter-born sheep. And as a result of this Anne trusts people will not say about her that she is strict with her husband, and Per cannot do anything but admit to himself 'It is for the best that Anne rules.'

149 What I have told you about Per and Anne is not an actual story, but in the presentation I have chosen to use I have joined together a great deal of the experiences that I have had in travelling amongst the people, regarding the habits and ways of thought of the working class. What I especially would emphasize for the benefit of the people in more cultivated classes is that remarkably great freedom which is found in the girl's relationship with the boy. One can anticipate, what experience also establishes, that when there is such great freedom it more frequently happens that less modest girls overstep the recognized border of what is decent which, as we have said, is also firmly fixed here. I refer to a case such as that of a girl who, at a young and unsettled age, loses her honour and as a result gives herself up to a more and more wanton life, with the abominable plan that, since the father of her first child deceived her, probably the second or the third child's father will in his turn be caught by her and become her husband. It is just the girl who has lost her character and becomes despised who has a double reason to dread lonely old age. She probably feels, therefore, that she has a kind of right to seek a breadwinner. I believe that many could verify that such cases are not unknown and that, when the depraved girl achieves her aim, one will certainly often find that it is an inexperienced young boy she has caught in her net. But each time that occurs it contributes to producing the condition that our statistics have shown, namely that so often in the working class it is young boys and older girls who marry.

150 In the attempt of the last few pages to find an explanation for the material presented in Tables 30, 31, and 32, the essay has expanded into a general consideration of certain aspects of the life of the people. But this fits our purpose quite well. No doubt the book is chiefly of a statistical nature, but the purpose of giving statistical information about the condition of the population is so that this will guide our investigations into the lives of the people. Since the comments just reported on, and the description of, the lives of the people serve to explain that

difference between the upper and lower classes which the tables brought
to our attention, those same tables serve, in some degree, to confirm our
interpretation of the circumstances and customs of the people.[13] So I
anticipate that it will be admitted that this present section bears a close
affinity to the essay as a whole. For like me the reader must have found
that, by putting oneself into the circumstances of the poor, one is less
inclined to subscribe to that frequently uttered proposition as to their
reckless marriages, a proposition which I have already rejected in the
introductory chapter.

At this juncture I must explain a particular point in this section. I
have talked here about night courtship. I have even portrayed night
courtship more straightforwardly than has been done, so far as I know,
in any other writing. It is not without misgiving that I have done so.
Nightly visits and night courtship seem indecent to townspeople, as
indecent (so strangely different can notions be) as a kiss between engaged or married people is for country folk in our land. In the countryside I can condemn night courtship in the strongest language without
anyone understanding me. In the town I must think twice before men-
tioning it, so as not to give the impression of going too far. It is therefore only after careful deliberation that I have spoken about the matter.
Whether the thing is considered indecent or not, it does no good to
pretend it does not exist. For one knows what misfortune must result
from the fact that each year 4,000 illegitimate children are born in our
country, and that an unknown, but pretty certainly a considerable
number of people are obliged to marry early and in poverty just to
conceal the shame of their loose living. These misfortunes, to a great
extent, must be attributed to the ancient custom of nightly visits in the
country districts where they prevail. If the custom – no, if this bad custom – is to be understood, it must be talked about and written about so
fully and so explicitly that it will be generally known and properly

[13] Regarding this, I ought not to conceal the fact that the explanations I have
given do not suffice to answer all the questions to which the tables give rise. One
such question is this: Why is it that the age difference between bride and bridegroom in each of the two classes is greater in the Christiansand than in the
Christiania Diocese (see Table 32)? According to the explanation given in paragraph 145, one might guess that one such reason is that the woman's position is
somewhat different in the two dioceses, to the extent that in the first she was not
so demeaned as to be considered a 'working person'. But if I dare to judge from
my own experience in some districts of the Christiansand Diocese (Lister and
Mandal counties, where the women, quite frequently, must share in such heavy
work as haymaking and thrashing corn), then I would sooner say that quite the
opposite takes place. What other circumstances there are which, in spite of this,
cause the greater age difference in the Diocese of Christiansand is not clear to me.
This then is something which I must leave for further enquiry.

understood. This is not the case at the moment. For it is not understood, either by those who without further thought condemn it as indecent, or by those who share the habit and regard it as harmless. Many wholly admirable people in the countryside have become engaged and have remained engaged for many years in the manner we have just described. For, as a result of their entire upbringing and education, they have not thought about any other way. That is the custom. Many wholly honourable people have sought each other's acquaintance and won each other's confidence in just this way and by doing so have exposed themselves to a temptation that was too strong for flesh and blood. That is the bad custom. What then one must do is to show the great danger inherent in this practice. One must strive (after inculcating the meaning of the daily prayer 'Lord lead us not into temptation') to raise the youth of the common people of our countryside to such a level of education that they understand correctly the difference between sensuality and love. For sensuality naturally sneaks in during the darkness of the night. On the other hand the young man who is clearly conscious that it is love which stirs in his breast does not shun the light of the sun.

The old institution of night courtship is as important a matter as it is complex. There are a multitude of conditions to be taken into account if one would correctly place it in the habits of the rural population. There are many differences in its practice in the different districts of the countryside. Here is not the place to deal with all of this. I would only add that I have reason to believe that recently, in some places, public opinion has begun to turn slightly against the good and the bad in night courtship. But the fact that the custom is changing by itself for the better is the greatest of challenges for a serious effort to be made to quicken the change. For now there is a greater hope than earlier that efforts in this matter will not be fruitless.[14]

---

[14] How the ways of thought and habits can, little by little, change for the better, I can best show by some words of a thoughtful farmer's wife, with whom I talked about this matter. It was in Romerike, in one of the country districts, where immorality is worst. The woman had herself been engaged in the way I have explained, and at the time thought no more about it. But since then, as a mistress with several servants under her, she had had an opportunity to see the tragic consequences of this nuisance and as a mother with grown-up children she had learned to fear the dangers involved. She expressed herself with great reluctance against the old way, but she also believed that it had declined somewhat, and added, 'And in ten years I am certain it will be abolished.' 'But on what do you base this belief?' I asked. 'I shall explain,' she continued. 'There are so many things that are different now from what they were before. It comes through the fact that we live so close to the town, where nearly every one of us has acquaintances or relatives whom we sometimes visit – for it is not so difficult to make a

151 In our days it is becoming more and more usual in writings of different kinds to illustrate the explanations that are given with pictures. I too have ventured to illustrate some of the propositions in this book with pictures in words or stories from real life. In this way I had originally thought to add a couple of further examples to show the meaning of the propositions given in paragraph 149. But when they were put on paper I found them too obnoxious to appear in this book. I have therefore omitted them. On the other hand, I will give here an illustration which is well suited to rendering intelligible a sensible practice which, in paragraph 146, I spoke of having found amongst the working class.

It is Jacob Shoemaker – he wasn't really called Jacob – whose lively story I shall give as literally as possible, though I shall deliberately change the names of the people concerned. Jacob Shoemaker is a fine man, whom I call my good friend. For still after many a long day I am happy to recall the many pleasant conversations we have had together and the happy afternoons I once spent in his house. But when I present him to the reader I ought perhaps to explain that he was such a shoemaker that he himself wore most of the shoes he sewed. He was an excellent and industrious farmer on his small freehold. Evidence of that was apparent from the great heap of stones by the side of his small patch of arable land. He was something of a businessman too, his business lying across the mountains between Gudbrandsdalen and the fjords of the Bergen Diocese. He was a hunter and in autumn went about the mountains after reindeer. Shoemaking was only a sideline which was

trip to town once in a while. But in that way new customs come into the parish. For instance it has recently become the fashion to hold parties, little dances, to which we ask some of our friends. My husband and I have done it for some years, and several others likewise. But now I see clearly that it is good for young people to come together in this way. In my youth it was the case that when young people, boys and girls, were together at some gathering – a funeral, or such like – then it was not done for us to even look at each other. That's how modest we were meant to be. The boys were expected to stick to one corner of the room, and the girls the other. Now, on the other hand, so far as I can see, boys and girls are able to be together and talk with each other and joke and laugh just as in town. It is as if they had just learned how. But you can be sure that when they have learned this, they won't fly together at night. They begin to be ashamed of it once they have learned the town ways. Now these were probably farmers' children, but it is the case that the crofter class are keen to take after the farming people. And besides I have thought – and talked with some of the other farmers' wives who will do the same – about holding a party for the servant people, now and then, such as on a Sunday evening, where they can enjoy themselves together and I can be present. My husband doesn't think much of the idea, for he is somewhat sharp and hard himself; but I am determined, and I mean to go through with it.'

good to turn to in between times. But the fact that he was a shoemaker meant that he did his work in the farmers' houses, as is the way in the countryside. This together with his other business interests must have contributed to his being so remarkably well known by everyone in the district. Indeed I made his acquaintance because I lived for some days on a farm where he happened to be doing some shoemaking. I made use of the opportunity and, not once but many times, got him to lay down his leather apron and accompany me for a stroll in the fields where we could talk freely.

'Listen to me, Jacob', I once said, after a whole lot of small talk 'You have explained so many things to me that I can but marvel. You have given me a better understanding of several matters concerning the way of life of people in a mountainous district like this. But now I'll mention something else. If you can explain this to me, I shall call you master. Yesterday evening we talked about marriage, but only fairly briefly. I want to know all about it because I fear that there are some who marry recklessly, in particular, naturally, such as come of poor people – such as you and your kind, Jacob. Don't you agree?'

'There is too much of it', answered Jacob.

'Now listen to what it is I want to ask you about. I have gone so far in this matter myself, that I have written to every single priest in the whole of the Christiania and Christiansand dioceses and asked them for several pieces of information from their parish registers. When I had put together all that the priests gave me, I found, first of all, something that I had expected, namely that the sons of crofters, servant-boys and such are quicker to marry than the sons of farmers. But then I found another thing which to me is so remarkable, namely that the poor boys who marry at the youngest age usually take as wives girls who are some years older. It is this which I now want to ask you about. How does it come about?'

'Ah! It could well be in many ways', said Jacob.

'Yes, one way is that the poor boy is such a scamp that he marries an older girl in order to get the *shillings* she has collected – what do you think about that?'

And Jacob would not deny that at times it could happen like that.

'But', he added, 'there is not now so much of that.'

'How did it happen then?'

'It has often been the case that when such a boy thinks of marrying, he must find someone who can manage well both in the house and in the byre. And it is easy then to understand that a young girl who has not long been in service has not so much of a knack of things as one who has worked for a long time under a good mistress.'

'And you mean to say that the boys think rationally in that way?' I asked in a doubting tone.

'Yes, I mean that', answered Jacob with a certain asperity. 'For, on the one hand, it is a fact that I myself have been a servant-boy and married, and on the other, that when people here in the neighbourhood think about getting married I nearly always know about it. I don't ask about it but all the same I know. I don't know how it happens.'

'So?'

'It happened once, I was shoemaking at this same farm where I am sewing now, that Ole, the crofter's son from Vasenden, came into the room. He sat on a bench and spoke for a bit with the people there. But I soon gathered that it was me he wanted to have a talk with. So he came to me and said, "Jacob," he said, "Come with me behind the barn." I put down my work and went with him. It turned out he wanted me to go down to Rognlien and propose to Marit for him. She was a servant there. I couldn't say anything else but yes, and indeed I said yes immediately, for I knew Marit and I knew she was a fine girl. "But tell me, Ole", I said, "I think it is strange that you should want to go just to her, for you are now not much over 20, and she is well over 30. It is so lop-sided." But Ole explained – and I couldn't say anything against it – that since it had now happened that he must take over a croft, for his father had become a widower and wanted to give it up, he needed to get someone to help him who really was able to manage animals and do all the other things. His relations had advised him to propose to Marit, who everyone knew was well thought of by her mistress, whom she had been under a long time. Ole also said that he had seen her on occasion, so they were not exactly strangers to each other. But he had not spoken to her about the matter and he thought that he could not bring himself to do so, for such a young lad is shy as you can well imagine.'

'Now tell me, Jacob, how did it go?'

'It went well. It was a Thursday, and on Saturday afternoon I had finished work really just for Ole's sake and went down to Rognlien. I went in the back way, for the byre is there. Marit was there too, for it was four weeks before Christmas and just at the time, towards the evening, when the animals are being seen to. But there was also a parish pauper in there who helped her carry water. So I said to Marit, "Marit, I want to have a word with you." When we had gone behind the barn, I told her what I'd come for and said what I had to say. I can't remember just how the words came, but she just stood and stared at me. "Answer me, Marit", I said. "Come with me up to the loft, Jacob", she said. When we had got up into the loft, where she had her chest, I was forced to sit down and drink a dram which she poured. And she gave me quite a thick piece of cake, so it seemed she was a prudent girl. And after a while she answered me. "Tell Ole from me that when he is at church next he can come in on his way home. And then he will get his answer." The next Communion Day we were at church, both Ole and I, and afterwards we went straight to the farm. Halvard Rognlien, the farmer there, stood out in the farmyard when we came. I was well known to him as I had grown up in this district. I understood that he knew the purpose of our visit, for as soon as he saw us he came and greeted us and had us into his living-room. Then we got coffee, both Ole and I. It was now the mistress of the house who treated us. For they expected us, as I saw that the coffee stood ready. After a while the husband led us into the parlour. He followed himself and a little while after Marit came in. There she stood so bashful and so shy and Ole, too, he couldn't say a word. So I had to say "Now we've come, as you see, Marit, to get the answer which you promised. So I ask you, Marit Hansdatter, if you have deliberated with your God and your heart and have in mind to have Ole Christensen Vasenden, who stands before you, as your bridegroom?" She shuffled her feet on the floor and didn't answer immediately. But then she lifted up her head and answered, so that we could just hear her, "Yes, so be it." And on this Ole and Marit took each other by the hand, and Halvard and I laid our hands over them, and so it was done. Then Marit went out and soon afterwards she came in again, with a bottle which contained a full half-pint and a plate with rum bread. First she served those of us who were in the parlour and then all the others who belonged to the house. So it was quite like a little party.'

'Ah, you are a splendid fellow for telling stories, Jacob!' I cried. 'But I must hear more. How did it go with Ole and Marit?'

'It went well. It is now three years since they came together and they live a good and prosperous life.'

'You must be an important person in the family. I suspect that you will have visited them sometimes?'

'Yes, I'm there often, for I have my mountain cabin and pasture up there where they live. So I visit frequently. And there is such a good feeling when I come in, that it's really marvellous. If I've not the time to wait while she puts on the coffee kettle then I must at any rate drink a glass of milk and eat a piece of cake, or whatever else it is Marit has to hand.'[15]

Thank you Jacob Shoemaker. Thank you for the story! It pleased me to hear it and it pleased me to recall it to mind. Stories of recklessness we hear everywhere, so it is pleasant, once in a while, to get true stories of circumspection and intelligence amongst the poor people also.

---

[15] I have told this courtship story as an example of sensible deliberation in the choice of a sweetheart. Ordinarily this is not the usual way to propose, and as some people draw the conclusion from the story that the kind of courtship with nightly visiting, which I spoke of earlier, might too not be so general as I presented it, then it cannot do harm to add that, from the same Jacob Shoemaker I heard a story, which, just at that time, had caused a great sensation in the district, and about which I have since got the complete picture; a story about a young couple who were engaged, though the boy did not visit the girl at night. This was due to the express demand of the girl's father and mother, farming people of otherwise simple habits, but highly regarded for their fear of God, and independent way of thinking. The stipulation was unheard of in the district, and opinion seemed to be divided as to its rightness, since some found it doubtful that the young people could 'conceive real love for each other in that way'.